Jesus
– a true story

Ruth Keable

Illustrations by Norman Hutton

Scripture Truth Publications

JESUS – A TRUE STORY

FIRST EDITION

FIRST PRINTING December 2006

ISBN-13: 978-0-901860-41-5

ISBN-10: 0-901860-41-7

© Copyright 2006 Scripture Truth

A publication of Scripture Truth

All rights reserved. No part of this publication may be reproduced, stored in a retrieval system, or transmitted, in any form or by any means, electronic, mechanical, photocopying, recording or otherwise without prior permission of Scripture Truth Publications.

Scripture quotations taken from the HOLY BIBLE,
NEW INTERNATIONAL VERSION.
Copyright © 1973, 1978, 1984 by International Bible Society.
Used by permission of Hodder & Stoughton Publishers,
A member of the Hodder Headline Group.
All rights reserved.
"NIV" is a registered trademark of International Bible Society.
UK trademark number 1448790.

Published by Scripture Truth Publications
Coopies Way, Coopies Lane,
Morpeth, Northumberland, NE61 6JN

Scripture Truth is an imprint of
Central Bible Hammond Trust, a charitable trust

Typesetting by John Rice
Printed by Lightning Source

NOTE TO READERS

You may wish to check out this story against the original: the Bible. To help you do this, references are provided to the relevant book, chapter and verse of the Bible in the form (book chapter:verse). For example, the reference at the end of the following quotation is to the gospel of John, chapter 20 and verses 30 and 31: "Jesus did many other miraculous signs in the presence of his disciples, which are not recorded in this book. But these are written that you may believe that Jesus is the Christ, the Son of God, and that believing you may have life in his name" (John 20:30-31).

When Jesus was born, he was declared to be "Christ the Lord" (Luke 2:11). For this reason many Christians refer to Jesus as "the Lord", and this title is used interchangeably with the name "Jesus" in the text.

Where a term requires further explanation, this is given in a note in a separate section, grouped by chapter, at the end of the book. In each chapter, its notes are enclosed in square brackets; for example, [2] in chapter 1 would refer to note 2 for that chapter.

JESUS – A TRUE STORY

CONTENTS

Chapter 1 7

Chapter 2 16

Chapter 3 27

Chapter 4 45

Chapter 5 58

Chapter 6 67

Chapter 7 76

Chapter 8 94

Bibliography 103

Notes 105

ISRAEL AND ITS NEIGHBOURS AT THE TIME OF JESUS

Chapter One

Mary and Joseph were an ordinary Jewish couple who lived in Nazareth, a quiet little town in the hills of Galilee. They were engaged to be married, and, in those days, this was a solemn commitment. Any breach of it was classed as adultery, and it could only be ended by divorce. One night, God sent the angel Gabriel to visit Mary. "Greetings, you who are highly favoured! The Lord is with you," he said (Luke 1:28). Mary was understandably startled, and so Gabriel told her not to be afraid for she had found favour with God. She had been chosen to bear a son, and she was to call him Jesus. "He will be great and will be called the Son of the Most High. The Lord God will give him the throne of his father David, and he will reign over the house of Jacob for ever; his kingdom will never end" (Luke 1:32-33). The angel was telling Mary to expect a very special baby. Mary was probably only a teenager, but she handled the situation remarkably well, no doubt on account of her strong faith. She believed what the angel had told her, but wondered how this was possible, for she was not yet married, and was still a virgin. The angel explained that her child would be conceived through the Holy Spirit, as this was God's Son, not Joseph's. He also told her that her cousin Elisabeth was six months pregnant, which was another miracle, as she was old, and infertile. We have to remember that nothing is impossible for God. It was true in the past and it is true now.

Mary immediately went to stay with Elisabeth, who lived in Judah. She had decided that it was best not to mention to Joseph about her meeting with the angel. She would tell him later. When Mary entered Elisabeth's house, she greeted her cousin. Elisabeth's baby leaped in her womb, and the Holy Spirit led her to declare that Mary was going to be the mother of the Lord. She felt privileged to have her in the house. The two women then spent several happy weeks talking about their expected babies. They were both very special babies; Mary's was the promised Messiah, and Elisabeth's would tell the people that Jesus was coming soon and he would baptise them. Elisabeth was the mother of John the Baptist. The two women were able to reassure each other, and they praised God together for his goodness. Mary left just before Elisabeth had her baby and she returned to Nazareth, and went to find Joseph.

Joseph was devastated when he found out that Mary was pregnant. He did not believe Mary's story about the angel, or the conception being due to the Holy Spirit. He decided to divorce her quietly, to cause as little upset as possible, but Mary was upset. She knew that she had told Joseph the truth. Joseph wanted to believe her but he just couldn't, so to reassure him, the Lord sent him a dream. In the dream, Joseph saw an angel, who told him to go ahead with his marriage to Mary. She had been telling the truth. She would have a son, but this was God's Son, and he was to be called Jesus. The angel reminded Joseph that the prophet Isaiah foretold that this would happen, years before. "The virgin will be with child, and will give birth

CHAPTER ONE

to a son, and they will call him Immanuel" (Isaiah 7:14). When he awoke, Joseph felt much better, and he and Mary were married shortly afterwards.

A few months later, not long before the baby was due, Joseph and Mary had to travel down to Judea. The Romans were compiling a register of all the people in their empire, and everyone had to go to the town or city nearest to where their family was from. Joseph and Mary were both descendants of David, and Bethlehem was the place where they had to go. It was five miles south of Jerusalem. They may have been relieved to get away from Nazareth for a while, as it is unlikely that many people there believed that Mary was still a virgin. The plan may have been to settle in Bethlehem, and have a fresh start there. The journey from Nazareth to Bethlehem took three days on foot, and maybe longer if the winter weather was bad. When at last they arrived at their destination, probably late in the day, they could not find any accommodation. The town was full of people like themselves, who had come to register their names, and all the available rooms were occupied. However, one kind innkeeper allowed Joseph and Mary to shelter in his stable. It was here, on a cold December night [1] that Mary gave birth to her son. She wrapped him in some cloths, and laid him down to sleep in a manger, which was an animals' feeding trough. The Son of God had been born in the humblest of circumstances.

In some nearby fields, a group of shepherds were watching over their sheep [2]. Suddenly an angel came to them, and they felt the glory of the Lord all around them. They were terrified. "Do not be afraid. I bring you good news of great joy that will be for all the people. Today in the town of David a Saviour has been born to you; he is Christ the Lord" (Luke 2:10-11). The angel told the shepherds to go and see the baby. They were to look for a new baby wrapped in swaddling clothes and lying in a manger. (Swaddling clothes were strips of cloth, which were used to wrap tightly round the baby to keep it warm and secure.) Then the shepherds heard a host of angels praising God and saying, "Glory to God in the highest, and on earth peace to men on whom his favour rests" (Luke 2:14). The shepherds listened and watched, and when the angels had gone, they thought they had better go into Bethlehem and see this baby in the manger. They went quickly and soon found the stable where Mary and Joseph were sheltering. After spending some time there, they departed, and told everyone about what they had seen that day. The news spread round the town, but Mary went over the events of the day in her mind. The Lord had been given a thoughtful and sensitive mother.

Although they knew Jesus was a special baby, Mary and Joseph were going to raise him in the normal Jewish way. This meant that when he was eight days old, he had to be circumcised. His name was officially given to him at this time too. There were certain Jewish ceremonial laws to be followed after the birth of a baby, so Mary, Joseph and the baby Jesus went to the temple at Jerusalem. Mary had to be "purified" after giving birth, which involved the offering of two sacrifices. A lamb could be offered if she could afford it, but because she was poor, Mary was allowed to offer two turtledoves or pigeons. As Jesus was the firstborn son in the family, he had to be presented to the Lord, then "redeemed", or bought back, for five silver shekels.

While they were in the temple, they met a man called Simeon. He was a devout Jew and knew the scriptures well. He was looking forward to the coming of the Messiah. God had told him through the Holy Spirit that he would not die until he saw him. Today the Holy Spirit

CHAPTER ONE

had led Simeon into the temple where the infant Jesus was. He took the baby in his arms and praised God for his goodness in sending his son to be the Saviour of the world. He could now die in peace. Simeon spoke to Mary and Joseph, then, he left. Watching all this was an elderly widow called Anna. Her husband had died many years ago, but she had found comfort in coming to the temple every day. She walked over to Mary and Joseph, and she too gave thanks to God. When she left, she told her friends about what had taken place in the temple that day.

Joseph managed to find a place for his family to live, and they settled down to life in Bethlehem. Meanwhile, a group (not necessarily only three) of wise men in the East (perhaps Arabia) had noticed a bright shining star in the sky. They were interested in the study of the stars, and this particular one had caught their attention. We know from history that the Jewish faith had travelled east, so perhaps this influence had led the wise men to the conclusion that this star signified the coming of the Jewish Messiah. They decided to make the journey to Jerusalem, where they hoped to find out where exactly this baby king was. By the time they reached Jerusalem and the court of King Herod the Great, the star had been shining for two years. They asked Herod where the Jewish King had been born. Herod was greatly troubled by this, for he was the king, and he certainly did not want any young pretender coming along to challenge his position. He called together the local Jewish High Priests and scribes, and asked them where they expected their Messiah to be born. (He didn't tell them that he had already been born.) They replied that according to the scriptures (Micah 5:2) they were expecting their king to be born in Bethlehem. Herod went back to the wise men. In order to establish how old this child was, he asked them when they had first seen the star in the sky. They told him that it was two years ago, so now Herod knew that the child could be no more than two years old. Herod directed the wise men to Bethlehem, and said he would be pleased if they could let him know when they found the child, as he wanted to worship him also. The wise men did not see the pretence in Herod's words, but departed joyfully for Bethlehem. The star led them right to the house where Jesus was. They worshipped him, and presented him with their gifts of gold, frankincense and myrrh. These gifts seem strange objects to give to an infant, but they were no doubt the finest products their country had to offer. These gifts are also symbolic. Gold was a gift for a king, which reminds us that Jesus is the King of the Jews. Frankincense was a vegetable resin, which gave off a perfume when burnt. It was used in the temple offerings, so this reminds us that Jesus is the Son of God. Myrrh was kept for a person's burial, so this reminds us that Jesus died for us.

The wise men had been asked to return to Herod, but God was not going to allow this, so he warned them in a dream. The next day, they returned home directly, avoiding any contact with Herod. Joseph too had a dream, in which an angel told him to take his family and go and live in Egypt for a while. This was because God knew that Herod was going to try to find Jesus and kill him. God knows what is going to happen to all of us in the future. Joseph did not hesitate to obey, and they left Bethlehem, and headed for Egypt. Herod waited for the wise men to return, but they never came. He was extremely angry, and very worried. He was determined that this child would not survive, so he ordered the killing of all the children under two in Bethlehem and the surrounding area [3]. Herod thought that this would solve his problem. His orders were carried out, and although he

CHAPTER ONE

had a cruel reputation, this awful deed must have shocked the quiet little town. Jesus, however, was safe. God had watched over him and protected him and his family.

Sometime later, Herod died, and so it was safe for Jesus to return to Israel. The angel came once again to Joseph in a dream, reassuring him that there was no danger to Jesus now. Joseph planned to settle in or around Bethlehem, but on hearing that Archelaus (one of Herod's sons) was now king of Judea, he changed his mind. If he was hesitating as to where to go now, God sent him another dream (his fourth). In this dream, God told him to go back to Galilee, and Joseph obeyed. They settled in their own hometown of Nazareth, and Jesus grew up there. We know practically nothing of his childhood, except that he "grew and became strong; he was filled with wisdom, and the grace of God was upon him" (Luke 2:40).

Galileans were generally regarded as ignorant, unlearned people, while Judeans were known for their education and wisdom. Galileans were fishermen or farmers, whereas Judea was the home of the intellectuals. It was amongst Galileans that Jesus grew up as a perfect child. Jewish children were taught all about their faith, first by their mother, then by their father. They were taught about the Jewish festivals, and they learned passages from the Bible, prayers and hymns. Later, at about six years old, they went to school. We do not know that there was a school in Nazareth at that time but, if there was, the young Jesus would have attended. What we do know is that, by the time he was twelve years old, he was very well taught in the scriptures.

When a Jewish boy was thirteen years old, he became of age, and was required by their law to observe personally the various Jewish feasts. In preparation for this, Joseph decided to take Jesus to the Passover feast when he was twelve years old. Mary was not legally required to attend in person, but she was happy to accompany them. The Passover feast was when Jews celebrated their deliverance from slavery in Egypt, and looked forward to the coming of the Messiah, or King of the Jews. Jesus was their Messiah. The feast took place in March or April, and many Jews travelled to Jerusalem to celebrate the Passover there.

The young Jesus must have been pleased to see the temple at Jerusalem, not just because it was so beautiful, but because it was his Father's house. The Passover feast lasted for a week, but the first two days were the most important. After this, the pilgrims could return home if they wanted, and it was at this stage that Joseph decided to take his family back to Nazareth. They were travelling in a large group that included their family and friends. Both Mary and Joseph assumed that Jesus was somewhere in the group, but he wasn't. He had remained in the temple. On a Feast day, such as this, the Doctors of the Law would teach the people on the temple terrace, and on this day, Jesus sat amongst the audience. He was not just listening, he was asking questions too. Everyone was amazed at the understanding of this young boy. When Joseph and Mary eventually found Jesus (three days after they had first realised he was missing), they too were amazed at what he knew. They were relieved to see him, but reproached him for causing them so much worry. Jesus answered calmly that he was doing his Father's work. He now realised that the purpose of his life was to see to his Father's business, and he committed himself to that for the rest of his life. Mary and Joseph were confused, as they did not fully understand their son, but Mary never forgot this day, and thought about it from time to time. Jesus

CHAPTER ONE

obediently left the temple, and travelled back to Nazareth with his family, where he continued to grow and mature into a young man. Mary and Joseph also had children of their own, so these would be stepbrothers and sisters for Jesus.

Chapter Two

Eighteen years went by. Palestine was now divided into four regions, with a ruler over each. Pontius Pilate (a Roman) governed Judea, and Herod Antipas (one of the sons of Herod the Great) ruled over Galilee and Perea. Another of Herod's sons, Philip, governed Iturea and Trachonitis (east of the river Jordan), and the small territory of Abilene was governed by Lysanias. These were the rulers while Jesus carried out his three years of public ministry.

John the Baptist was six months older than Jesus was. He was now living primitively in the wilderness in Judea. His food was locusts and wild honey, and he made his clothes out of camels' hair, because he had no money. He had given up all home comforts, because he had a mission. This was to prepare the people for the coming of the Messiah. He told them that Jesus would soon be with them, and they should prepare themselves for his coming and repent of their sins. To show this to everyone they should be baptised, and John would do this for them in the river Jordan. Life was difficult for the people at the time, due to oppression by the Romans. It was also a time of spiritual decline, a case of every man for himself, so as

CHAPTER TWO

a result there was a lot of unhappiness about. Many people were interested in what John had to say, and came to listen to him in the wilderness. Many were baptised, and gave up their wicked ways. Some even thought that John was the Messiah, but he immediately put them right about that, saying that he was not even worthy enough to untie Jesus' shoes.

It was now early in the year, perhaps late January, and Jesus was thirty years old. John the Baptist had moved north, and was baptising people at Bethabara, also known as Bethany beyond the Jordan. This place was somewhere just north of the Dead Sea. When Jesus heard that John was there, he left Nazareth and headed south to Bethabara. He wanted to be part of this. He had no need of repentance, as he was sinless, but being baptised was the right thing for a Jew to do, so he would do it. It would mean the end of his private life and the beginning of his public one. When Jesus arrived at the water's edge, John did not know who he was at first, even though they were related. They must have had no contact while they were growing up. Once he did realise who this man was, John refused to baptise him, because he did not think he needed it. Furthermore John rightly considered that, as a person, he, John, was much less worthy than Jesus. Jesus, however, insisted that John baptise him, and so he did. When he came out of the water, the heavens opened, and the Spirit of God descended upon him in the form of a dove. A voice from heaven was heard, saying, "This is my Son, whom I love; with him I am well pleased" (Matthew 3:17). This was the first of three occasions when God spoke in an audible voice about his Son.

Immediately after this, the Holy Spirit led Jesus into the wilderness, probably somewhere near Jericho. God was going to put him through a time of testing. He remained there for forty days and nights, and purposely went without food during this time. He was preparing for his public ministry. God allowed Satan to come and tempt him, but although Jesus was physically weak from his fasting, he did not give in to the temptations. He couldn't have, because he was God's Son, and was incapable of sinning. Satan knew that Jesus was hungry, so he suggested that he turn stones into bread. Jesus answered, "Man does not live on bread alone, but on every word that comes from the mouth of God" (Matthew 4:4). Then Satan took Jesus to the top of the temple, and told him to throw himself off, and angels would catch him. Jesus answered, "Do not put the Lord your God to the test" (Matthew 4:7). Satan also took him up a high mountain and showed him all the kingdoms of the world, promising to give them to Jesus, if he would worship him. Jesus answered, "Away from me, Satan! For it is written: 'Worship the Lord your God, and serve him only'" (Matthew 4:10). Jesus had answered each temptation with a quotation from the Bible. He had not sought to get out of the situation; he had endured the trial and submitted to the will of God. Satan had failed, so he left Jesus alone for a while. Jesus was weak from his ordeal, but angels came to minister to him.

Jesus returned to Bethabara on a Friday, and saw John the Baptist. The next day, the Sabbath [1], Jesus went down to the river to see John again. Two of John's disciples, John and Andrew, heard Jesus speaking, and began to follow him from that moment. They and their brothers (James and Peter) spent that day with Jesus. James and John were

CHAPTER TWO

Jesus' cousins through their mother. Their mother was Salome, who was the sister of Mary, the mother of Jesus. Peter and Andrew were also brothers, and worked with James and John as fishing partners.

The next day, Sunday, was when Jesus began his mission work. He set off from Bethabara with his first four disciples and travelled towards Galilee. On the way, they met Philip, a probable acquaintance of Andrew and Peter. (They were from the same town.) He joined them, and told his friend Nathaniel (sometimes called Bartholomew) that they had found the Messiah. He also joined the group, so now there were six disciples.

It took three days to reach Cana in Galilee. Cana was on the road from Nazareth to Tiberias. They arrived in time for a wedding on the Wednesday. Jewish tradition was for young girls to be married on Wednesdays while widows were married on Thursdays. Nathaniel lived in Cana, so it is possible that Jesus and the other five disciples stayed at his house. They were all invited to the wedding, where Jesus performed his first miracle, the turning of water into wine. This might have been the wedding of a member of Jesus' family, as his mother Mary was involved in the arrangements. During the wedding feast, Mary told Jesus that there was no wine left. To save any embarrassment, Jesus agreed to help. Mary instructed the servants to do whatever he told them. Jesus asked them to fill six water pots with water, which they did.

Then he told them to pour a cup out and give it to the governor of the feast. Again, they obeyed without question or argument. Jesus had turned the water into wine, and good wine too. He had saved the day, and the disciples had seen it all. It helped confirm to them that Jesus was truly the Son of God. After the wedding, Jesus went to Capernaum for a few days with his mother and brothers and the six disciples. Peter lived here, although he was originally from Bethsaida, a town further round Lake Galilee. Capernaum became the base for much of the Lord's ministry.

The Passover season was now approaching, so Jesus and the disciples set off for Jerusalem, a distance of about eighty miles. On entering the temple, Jesus was angry about the corruption he found there. Traders had set up a market stall to sell animals for the temple sacrifices, but they were swindlers, and cheated the people. Jesus made a scourge and drove all the people out, overturning their tables. No one tried to stop him. Perhaps their consciences told them he was right. Here Jesus had his first encounter with the Jewish authorities, the first of many. As was usually the case, they didn't understand what he was talking about. The disciples however showed signs of spiritual understanding already. They could relate things they had read in the Old Testament, to the things that Jesus did and said. Jesus performed many miracles here, and many people believed in him, but he did not say too much at this early stage, as he knew that most of them just wanted to see miracles. However, there were exceptions.

One person, who had seen the miracles and believed, was Nicodemus, a ruler of the Jews. He came to see Jesus one night, and Jesus spent a long time with him, explaining many things. This was in contrast to the crowd, who were only interested in the miracles. Here was someone who was interested in what Jesus had to say. It was to

CHAPTER TWO

Nicodemus that Jesus explained the need to be born again (John chapter 3).

Jesus remained in Jerusalem for a little while longer, and then he headed north with his disciples. On the way, he stopped to teach people, and the disciples baptised. The Jews were not happy about this, so Jesus and the six disciples left the area and headed north to Samaria. It was at this time that Herod Antipas, ruler of Galilee, imprisoned John the Baptist.

It was now about the middle of May. The road through Samaria was difficult and at Sychar, where there was a well, Jesus stopped for a rest. It was six o'clock in the evening and the disciples had gone to the town to buy food [2]. A Samaritan woman came to the well for water, and Jesus asked her if she would give him a drink. He talked to her for some time about who he was, and he made it clear that he knew all about her, and her past. When the disciples came back, they were amazed that Jesus was talking to this woman, as Jews did not get on with Samaritans. However, they did not dare say anything, but tried to get him to have some food. Jesus gave the impression that he was more interested in his work; that is, in people's souls, than food, something the disciples failed to understand at this point. The woman must have immediately told all her friends and neighbours about Jesus and very quickly, they came out to see him for themselves. There is no mention of miracles here (see John chapter 4); the Samaritans only seemed interested in what Jesus had to say, and many believed in him. They begged him to stay with them, so Jesus stayed there for two days, after which he had to leave for Galilee.

Jesus said at this point that a prophet has no honour in his own country so, after being accepted in hostile Samaria, he headed for his own country of Galilee. The disciples must have gone back to their own homes now, as there is no mention of them for a while. When Jesus reached Galilee his fame had already spread from Jerusalem where many had seen him. His first stop was Cana, where he had been for the wedding. While he was here, a nobleman came to him from Capernaum, a distance of about 25 miles. This man was most probably a court official at the court of Herod Antipas, ruler of Galilee. He begged Jesus to heal his son, who was at the point of death. Jesus did so, proving that he could heal from a distance. This might have been the family spoken of in Luke 8:3, the man being Herod's steward and the wife being one of the women who ministered to the Lord. What we do know is that the whole family believed in Jesus because of these events.

The next event is when Jesus returned to his home town of Nazareth. It was the Sabbath and he went into the synagogue there and taught from the scriptures. However, he was not well received by his own townspeople, just as he had remarked back in Samaria. He now makes a similar comment. "No prophet is accepted in his home town" (Luke 4:24). In fact, they tried to kill him by pushing him over a 40-foot cliff, but he calmly walked away from them and made his way to Capernaum, alone.

It was here that Jesus made his Galilean home and not in Nazareth. Simon Peter lived here, as did the newly converted household of the court official whose son Jesus had healed. Andrew, James and John lived close by. Jesus spent the summer in this area, teaching and healing; the disciples had not yet been officially called, so he must have been alone most of the time.

CHAPTER TWO

At the end of the summer, Jesus went to Jerusalem for a feast, described in John 5 simply as a feast of the Jews. There were several Jewish feasts throughout the year, and we are not told which one this was. Given the time of year, it might have been the Feast of Wood-Offering on the 15th August, or it might have been the Feast of Trumpets, which marked the beginning of the civil New Year. This fell in mid September [3]. While in Jerusalem, Jesus came across the pool of Bethesda. It was a bubbling spring of water, but the popular idea was that an angel came to stir up the water and the first one to step in after this, would be healed. Jesus saw a disabled man there. Jesus asked him if he wanted to be healed, which was unusual, as, normally, Jesus waited to be asked for healing. The man was healed without even going in the water and the news spread. Jesus saw this man later in the temple. He had obviously become a believer, and told everyone what Jesus had done for him. The Jews were not pleased because it was the Sabbath day. They did not think that Jesus ought to heal on this day, so they began to persecute him. He answered them, "My Father is always at his work to this very day, and I, too, am working" (John 5:17). By saying this, Jesus was calling God his father, which made him equal with God. The Jews did not accept this, and wanted to kill him for saying it, so Jesus left Jerusalem and went back to Galilee.

Jesus now went to call his disciples together officially, starting with the first four: Simon Peter, Andrew, James and John. He found them by the lake, mending their nets. He got into Simon Peter's boat and taught from there. Afterwards, they went further out to sea where Jesus told them to let down their nets. Simon Peter was surprised as they had caught nothing all night, but he obeyed nevertheless. Their nets became full so they had to ask James and John to help them. This had a great impact on them all, particularly Simon Peter and from this moment, they left everything and followed Jesus.

The following Sabbath day they all went to the synagogue at Capernaum where Jesus taught with authority. Everyone was amazed. They could see that Jesus knew what he was talking about, unlike the scribes. There was in the synagogue a man with an unclean spirit; that is, he was at that time demon possessed. Just as God was on earth in human form, so Satan came to attack the Lord's work by temporarily dwelling in man. However, Jesus had greater power and rebuked the spirit, which then left this man. The crowd were amazed, and the news spread round the whole country.

After this incident, Jesus and the disciples went to Peter's home. Peter lived with his wife and her mother, who was at this time ill with a fever. The disciples, knowing that Jesus could heal, asked him to have a look at her. Jesus rebuked the fever, just as he had rebuked the demon in the synagogue and immediately it left her. She was then able to prepare the Sabbath meal, which they could all enjoy together. The evening of the same day, many people came to Simon Peter's house to see Jesus, bringing with them sick friends and relatives. Jesus healed them all and cast out many demons that evening. It had been a long busy day but the next morning, somewhere between 3 and 6 o'clock, Jesus got up and went off alone to pray. The disciples, once they realised that Jesus was missing, followed on afterwards. They found Jesus and told him that many people wanted to see him, but Jesus told the disciples that they would have to move on, as there were other towns to

CHAPTER TWO

visit and so Jesus began another tour of Galilee. It was now autumn.

One of the first things we read about on this tour is the cleansing of a leper. At that time the rabbis were very hard on lepers, sometimes even throwing stones at them to keep them away. In contrast to this, the leper felt free to approach Jesus and humbly ask for cleansing. Jesus, moved with compassion, healed him immediately. He then told this man to report to the priest so that he could be declared clean, as this was a requirement of the law. He also told him to keep the matter quiet so as not to attract attention to himself. However the man told everyone what Jesus had done for him so they had to leave that city and withdraw to more deserted places. People still found him there, so Jesus had to explain that he had to preach in other cities, and so had to keep on the move.

Jesus spent the autumn travelling around Galilee and returned to Capernaum in the winter. One day Jesus was teaching in Peter's house. Many were gathered there to hear him, from every walk of life, including Pharisees [4] and Doctors of the Law and people from as far away as Jerusalem. Jesus was teaching in the covered gallery of the house, which was like a back yard with a simple, tiled roof. Four men had brought their bedridden friend to see Jesus, but, as the house was so crowded, they lowered him through the roof. Jesus could see how much faith they had and immediately forgave the man for his sins. The learned people in the crowd noticed this straight away, no doubt looking for faults, but Jesus could read their thoughts. It seems that after the first encounter with Jesus at the unknown feast in Jerusalem, back in the late summer, there were those sent out to spy on the Lord and see what he was up to. It was important for Jesus to forgive sins before healing, to show that he was God. He then confirmed this by the miracle of healing, which was of secondary importance. His main mission was to forgive sins, so, now his sins were forgiven, Jesus told the man to take up his bed and walk home. Many were impressed by this miracle, and glorified God.

Chapter Three

Some time later, probably early the next year, Jesus went again to the lake. (Lake Galilee is also referred to as the Sea of Galilee.) Levi (also called Matthew) must have heard Jesus many times when he was down at the seashore. Levi worked as a tax collector, collecting payments from people and ships crossing Lake Galilee. The public hated tax collectors because so many of them were dishonest. Levi worked in the Custom House, and these people were the most despised of all the tax collectors. Levi must have known the first disciples of Jesus, as they were local fishermen, and he would have seen what had been going on in the area over the last few months. He had no doubt thought over those events many times and looked at his own life. When Jesus came to him that day, to call him to discipleship, he did not hesitate. It seems that straight after this, Levi invited Jesus to his home for a meal, along with the disciples and some other tax collectors. This was noticed by the scribes [1] and Pharisees, and some of the disciples of John the Baptist. There was quite a lively discussion about why Jesus had come, but Jesus spoke in parables and some of them did not understand him.

It would appear that the other five disciples were called after this, making their number up to twelve.

They were:

>James
>John
>Simon Peter
>Andrew
>Philip
>Nathaniel also called Bartholomew
>Matthew also called Levi
>Thomas also called Didymus
>Judas Lebbaeus Thaddeus
>Simon the Zealot
>James
>Judas Iscariot.

It was probably on one of the mountains to the north of Capernaum that Jesus had spent a night of prayer. The next day he officially appointed the twelve as apostles. The multitudes soon found them, and many were healed that day. What seems to have happened is that Jesus and his twelve disciples eventually went back up the mountain. Jesus wanted to teach them all about the Kingdom of God. Some of the crowd followed them. This teaching has become known as the Sermon on the Mount, and would have been very different to the Jewish teaching they were used to. It can be found in Matthew chapters 5, 6, 7, and Luke chapter 6. This is where we also find what is often known as the "Lord's Prayer" (Matthew 6:9-15). It is interesting to note that references to lilies of the field suggest that this event took place in the spring. (Presumably, the Lord noticed them growing there and referred to them as an example.)

CHAPTER THREE

After this, they all came back down the mountain and entered Capernaum. The crowds soon gathered again, so much so that Jesus and the disciples did not even have time to eat. It was here that there came a request from a Gentile [2] centurion. This man had come to love Israel and respect their God. He had even built a synagogue for the Jews in Capernaum. As he was not a Jew himself, the centurion was reserved about asking Jesus to heal his servant. He was not sure if Jesus would heal a Gentile, so he sent Jewish elders to ask him. Jesus agreed to help, and set off towards the house. Before he got there, he received another message. The centurion felt that as a Gentile, he was unworthy, and he didn't want Jesus to be defiled by entering his home [3]. The message was for Jesus to give the word and heal the servant from a distance. Jesus was amazed at the faith he had found in this man and expressed this to those around him. The servant was healed.

The next day, a large crowd followed Jesus and the disciples to Nain, a distance of about 25 miles southwest of Capernaum. At the gate to this city, they met another crowd of people. This was a funeral procession for the only son of a widow. The Lord was moved to compassion by the sight of the widow weeping. "Don't cry", he said, and went over to the bier and touched it. He told the dead young man to arise, which he did and began to speak. Then Jesus took him over to his mother. There were many witnesses to this miracle of resurrection and they were all afraid. The news spread everywhere about the events of this day. News even reached John the Baptist in prison and he sent some of his disciples to ask Jesus if he was the one that should come, or were they to look for another. Jesus answered this by healing many sick people and telling John's disciples to go back and tell him what they had seen.

A Pharisee called Simon had invited Jesus to his house for a meal. As they were dining, an unnamed woman came into the house. She had no doubt heard the words of Jesus and realised that he was God's Son. In her hands, she carried an alabaster box containing precious ointment. She began to anoint the Lord's feet, weeping as she did so. This woman had led a sinful life, and this burden came before her at this moment. It must have been a very moving scene. Jesus broke the silence by addressing Simon. He had read his unspoken thoughts. Simon disapproved of what was happening because of the woman's sinful background. Jesus spoke to him with an illustration, to explain that people, who have sinned badly, really appreciate his forgiveness, and love him much in return. Simon had given the Lord a polite reception, whereas the woman had given him a very special, loving reception. Jesus then turned to the woman and reassured her that her sins had been forgiven. It seems that she was a believer already, but had lacked the peace of forgiveness because of her sinful life. The attitude of Simon the Pharisee reflected the growing opposition to Jesus, which had begun at the unspecified feast at Jerusalem.

Jesus continued his tour of Galilee accompanied by the twelve disciples and several women, including Mary Magdalene, Joanna and Susanna. These women had the privilege of caring for Jesus and the twelve, as they worked their way round Galilee, preaching and healing. There was some opposition from Pharisees and scribes from Jerusalem, particularly regarding the Lord's ability to cast out devils. An example of this was the healing of the demonised, dumb man in Matthew 12. They attributed his power to Satan. Because of this opposition to the

CHAPTER THREE

Lord's work, Mary the mother of Jesus, and her children, decided to visit him. They were probably concerned for his safety, but must have been surprised at the Lord's response. He did not leave what he was doing, as they might have expected, but told everyone that, whoever does his Father's will, they were his family. It was not that he did not respect his mother, but his relationship with God and his work came first.

By the time the tour of Galilee was over, it was late spring, just a few weeks before the Passover. Jesus continued to teach down by Lake Galilee. He began to speak in parables. Parables were illustrations Jesus gave to explain his teachings. They usually involved a simple story of an everyday situation. Jesus used them as the opposition from the Pharisees increased. The Pharisees did not understand them, because they did not have the faith. The Lord told three series of parables at different times in his life. The first series came at this time from a ship on Lake Galilee, addressed to the multitudes and the disciples. It was in response to Pharisaic opposition (when they attributed his power to Satan), and in response to the visit by Jesus' family, and concerns the planting of the Kingdom of God.

The parables are as follows:

The sower..Matthew 13:3-23, Mark 4:3-20, Luke 8:5-15

The mustard seed .... Matthew 13:31-32, Mark 4:30-32

The yeast ....Matthew 13:33

The weeds .... Matthew 13:24-30, Matthew 13:36-43

The growing seed ....Mark 4:26-29

It is interesting to note that the sower was the first parable and the Lord said about it, "Don't you understand this parable? How then will you understand any parable?" (Mark 4:13). The Lord spoke these parables without explanation, but the disciples were given further teaching on them privately, later.

They (the twelve) were also told three more parables at this time.

The hidden treasure .... Matthew 13:44

The pearl .... Matthew 13:45-46

The net .... Matthew 13:47-50

There were still crowds gathered by the time evening came, but Jesus asked the disciples to take their boat to the other side of Lake Galilee, which they did immediately. A few other boats followed too. Jesus was exhausted from his day of teaching and fell asleep in the boat. After a while, a storm came and the boat began to fill with water. The disciples were very frightened and woke Jesus up to help them. Jesus rebuked them for their lack of faith. He rebuked the waves and there was calm again. The disciples marvelled at his power. The little boat then sailed across Galilee to the Gadarene country in Decapolis, a short distance of four or five miles south east of Capernaum. It would not have taken long.

As soon as they had reached this place and had left the boat, two men rushed over to meet them. These men lived in the tombs there and were uncontrollable, because they were demon-possessed. One of the men ran up to Jesus and worshipped him and Jesus ordered the demons out of

CHAPTER THREE

the two men. The demons recognised the authority Jesus had and asked him if they could enter a herd of pigs nearby. Jesus allowed this and the herd went charging down the cliff and into the lake. They all drowned. The people who were with the herd rushed off to tell everyone in the city what had happened. However, their reaction was one of fear and they asked Jesus to leave. The men Jesus had helped begged him to stay but Jesus told them to go back home and tell their friends what had happened to them, then he left.

When Jesus and the disciples got back to Capernaum, there was already a crowd waiting, eager to see him. It was now morning. One person in the crowd was Jairus, a ruler of the synagogue. He approached Jesus, very distressed. His only child, a daughter aged twelve, was dying. He asked the Lord to come to his house and heal her. On the way to this house, Jesus met somebody else. There was a woman who had been suffering from severe bleeding for twelve years [4]. Perhaps she had heard that Jesus could heal from a distance, so she thought that if she could just touch his clothes, she would be healed. This is what she did and she was healed immediately. The Lord felt the power go out of him. She had not been healed because she had touched him but because she had faith in him. Jesus confirmed this when he spoke to her. He knew that she had touched him, but made her come out from the crowd and admit it.

All this time Jairus was waiting patiently for the Lord to go to his daughter, but now there was a message that she was dead. However, Jesus reassured Jairus and told him to believe and she would be made whole. Then he made the crowd stay where they were and he entered the house with Peter, James, John and the girl's parents. "The child is not dead but asleep," Jesus said (Mark 5:39), but the people who were stood there mourning only laughed at him. Then they went into the room where the little girl lay and Jesus brought her back to life. Jesus told them not to tell anyone what had happened, but the news soon spread from town to town.

After these events, the Lord was not seen in Capernaum to the same extent again, although he did visit from time to time. Having left Capernaum then, he travelled, with the twelve disciples, to Nazareth. Mark 6:3 suggests that of his earthly family, only the Lord's sisters remained in Nazareth now. They were no doubt married to Nazarenes. Mary and her sons seemed to have moved to Capernaum or nearby, presumably to be near Jesus. Joseph is not mentioned, so we assume that he had died.

It was the Sabbath day and Jesus went to the synagogue in Nazareth. The last time he was at this synagogue was about nine or ten months previously. He had been given a poor reception at that time. The people of Nazareth remembered Jesus and the family, and they had heard all about the miracles he had done. They listened to all that he had to say in the synagogue that day, and they were astonished. However, they did not believe in him, so Jesus did only a little work in Nazareth and then left there for good.

Now Jesus decided that it was time to send the twelve disciples on missionary journeys. He gave them some advice and instructions, and then sent them out in pairs, telling them to go to Jewish areas only this time. They were given power over demons and were able to heal the sick. Jesus himself also did some teaching and preaching in nearby cities, but he went alone. These missionary journeys could not have lasted for more than a couple of weeks, although it was long enough to attract the attention of Herod

CHAPTER THREE

Antipas. He was worried by their activities. He had just beheaded John the Baptist, and thought that he must have come back from the dead.

It seems that the murder of John brought the disciples back to Jesus. They had all had a very busy spring and the news of John's death must have been very upsetting. This was probably why Jesus took them all into the desert near Bethsaida to rest for a while. This was east of the Galilean region, and that meant outside the jurisdiction of Herod Antipas, therefore away from potential trouble. It was not long before the crowds found them again. Jesus and the twelve were in a boat and the crowd followed on foot. John 6:4 tells us that it was almost time for the Passover. Perhaps many were starting their journey round the lake then down through Perea and on to Jerusalem for the Passover. Soon there was a crowd of five thousand men, besides the women and children. Jesus took the disciples up a mountain, but they could see the crowd who had followed gathering on the plain below. Jesus was moved with compassion for them and went down to be with them, teaching and healing them. At the end of the day, the disciples urged Jesus to send the crowds away to buy food for themselves. However, Jesus had another idea and turned to Philip. "Where shall we buy bread for these people to eat?" Jesus asked him (John 6:5). He said this to test Philip, who was inclined to look at problems in a human, rather than a spiritual way. Philip tried to work out how much they would need to buy, but Andrew brought a boy to Jesus. This boy had only five loaves of barley bread (the food of the poor), and two small fish (probably dried or pickled sardines). Andrew was not sure whether this would help or not. He seemed to show partly belief, yet partly doubt. However, when Jesus asked the disciples to make the people sit down, they obeyed without question.

Mark 6 describes them as sitting in ranks of fifty or a hundred [5]. In a few weeks time, the green grass in this area would have dried up, so the mention of green grass confirms the time of year when this took place as just before the Passover (Mark 6:39). Jesus took the food and gave thanks to God for it. The disciples shared it round, and everyone had plenty to eat. There were even twelve full baskets left over. The crowd believed on him that day, and would have made him their king right then, but Jesus did not want this. He told the disciples to sail back over the lake towards Capernaum and he would follow later. He sent the multitude away and then went back up the mountain to pray, alone.

Meanwhile, a strong wind was blowing, and the disciples' little ship was in difficulties. Jesus saw them, but waited until the fourth watch (probably between 3 and 6 am), before he went to them, walking on the water. They all saw him but thought he was a ghost and were frightened. Jesus immediately spoke to them and told them to have no fear. Peter, perhaps with some doubt, said, "Lord, if it's you, tell me to come to you on the water" (Matthew 14:28). Jesus said, "Come", and so Peter walked to him on the water, but was soon overcome with fear. "Lord save

CHAPTER THREE

me," he cried. Peter seemed to have a mixture of doubt and faith going on in his mind. The Lord helped him, then they climbed into the boat. The disciples were amazed at what they had just witnessed. They seemed to have forgotten already that Jesus had miraculous power, even though they had just been part of the feeding of the five thousand. At this point, the wind died down, but the boat had blown off course, and they landed at Gennesaret, a few miles further round Lake Galilee, to the South West. It was now early Friday morning, and the party had only been on land for a short time, when the crowds came to see Jesus, bringing their sick friends with them. They travelled northwards towards Capernaum, in order to be in the synagogue there for the Sabbath. Pharisees and scribes from Jerusalem met them on the way. They started to find fault with Jesus over the fact that the disciples had eaten without washing their hands, but Jesus was able to answer them [6]. They may have heard about the feeding of the five thousand, and were looking to find fault. This subject was continued the next day, the Sabbath, in the synagogue. Jesus gave an address on traditionalism and defilement, basically saying that it was not outward things such as hand washing which affected a man, but his inner self – his heart and conscience. Jesus also explained this to the crowd gathered outside. Some of them had been part of the feeding of the five thousand, and had come to Capernaum to find Jesus. The Lord knew that there were many who were only interested in the loaves and fishes, and not in his teaching, so he spoke directly to the people that day. Jesus declared, "I am the bread of life. He who comes to me will never go hungry" (John 6:35). He was the answer to all their needs if only they would

37

accept him. As a result of his direct teaching, many stopped following him from then. It was at this point that Jesus asked his disciples if they would also go away. Peter replied, "Lord, to whom shall we go? You have the words of eternal life" (John 6:68).

After the Sabbath, Jesus and the twelve left Capernaum and arrived at a house in the borders of Tyre and Sidon, a region to the north of Galilee. This was the time when the Passover was taking place. It was a Jewish home, and Jesus had hoped to find peace and quiet there. He must have stayed there for a few days, and the news spread round the area that Jesus was there. A woman, described as a Syro-Phoenician, in other words a Gentile woman, was very interested that Jesus was in the area. She had a daughter who was demon-possessed, so she came to Jesus to ask him to help. She addressed Jesus as the 'Son of David', which was a Jewish expression. Jesus took up this theme and taught her that he had come to the Jews first, saying that it was not right to give the children's bread to dogs. At that time the Jews commonly called the Gentiles 'dogs'. Then the woman called him 'Lord' instead, and said, "But even the dogs under the table eat the children's crumbs" (Mark 7:28). This woman understood what Jesus was telling her, and wanted to share in his blessing. Jesus acknowledged her faith, and her daughter was healed.

Jesus then left this area and headed for Decapolis and the eastern shore of Lake Galilee. The route he took was probably east and then south. As the Passover had just taken place, the Jerusalem scribes and Pharisees were not present at this time. They were required to be in the temple at Jerusalem for the Passover celebrations. This accounts for their absence from the scene at the next group of miracles. Those specifically mentioned were the healing of a deaf and dumb man in Mark 7:32-37, the healing of a blind man in Mark 8:22-26 and the healing of two blind men in Matthew 9:27-31. The people in this area were heathens. This was perhaps why Jesus took more time over these miracles, for example, He looked up to heaven to show where his power came from. He touched the ears and tongue of the deaf and dumb man and the eyes of the blind men, to show them what he was going to do. After each of these miracles, Jesus told them to tell no one what had happened. Perhaps the Lord did not want to be hindered by crowds at this point. Soon after this, the Pharisees from Jerusalem arrived back on the scene. It was the Sabbath day, not long after the Passover. This had been the second Passover of the Lord's public ministry [7]. Matthew 12:1-21, Mark 2:23-3:6, Luke 6:1-11, give us the details of what happened after this second Passover although their placement in the gospels is not in chronological order but in relation to the Pharisees and their teaching.

On this Sabbath day, Jesus and the twelve disciples were walking through a cornfield. The Pharisees were following them. As the disciples were hungry, they began to eat some of the corn growing there. The Pharisees immediately began to condemn this action, as, to them, it broke the laws of the Sabbath [8]. Jesus answered them straight away, explaining that the disciples had not done anything wrong. They were serving the Lord, and if they were hungry, then Jesus wanted them to have food. He tried to explain what the Sabbath day was for, basically, a day for rest and worship, but the Pharisees did not accept this because they did not accept Jesus as God's Son.

It was probably the very next Sabbath that another controversy arose between Jesus and the Pharisees. They were all in the synagogue when the scribes and Pharisees noticed a man with a withered hand. They watched to see what Jesus would do. Would he heal him on the Sabbath? They hoped he would, so that they could accuse him of breaking the Sabbath laws. They had no concern for the man. Jesus knew what they were thinking and was angry about the hardness of their hearts. He told them that it was lawful to do good on the Sabbath, then he healed the man's hand. The Pharisees and scribes were very annoyed about this and started to plot with the Herodians [9] about how they might kill him.

For this reason, Jesus withdrew from this area to Gentile territory, probably Decapolis again. Crowds followed Jesus for three days, and were getting hungry. In a similar way to the feeding of the five thousand, Jesus provided food for the multitude, which in this case numbered four thousand men besides the women and children. There were seven loaves and a few little fish this time, and afterwards there were seven full baskets left over. This time the people sat on the ground. (The grass had dried up by this time of year.) These people were Gentiles, as opposed to the Jewish multitude of five thousand. Just as the feeding of the five thousand closed the Galilean ministry, the feeding of the four thousand closed the Lord's Decapolis ministry. Having dismissed the crowd, Jesus and the disciples got into a boat and sailed across Lake Galilee to Magadan (Matthew 15:39) and Dalmanutha (Mark 8:10).

CHAPTER THREE

Neither of these towns has been identified, but the area in question is thought to have been near Taricheae, on the west side of Lake Galilee. The Pharisees and Sadducees [10] heard they were there and came to cause trouble. They asked Jesus to show them a sign from heaven, but he wouldn't. Jesus then told them that although they could read the signs in the sky, they could not read the signs of the times. We still read the sky today. ("Red sky at night, shepherds' delight. Red sky at morning, shepherds' warning.") The Pharisees and Sadducees did not believe in him anyway, so a sign would not have changed anything.

After this, Jesus and the disciples got back into their boat and sailed across to the east side of the lake. When they got there, Jesus, perhaps still concerned about what had just happened, began to warn the disciples about the false teaching of the Pharisees, and said, "Watch out for the yeast of the Pharisees and that of Herod" (Mark 8:15). They thought he was talking about their supply of bread, as they were down to their last loaf. Considering all the time they had spent with Jesus, the disciples were sometimes slow to understand his teaching.

They travelled northwards to Caesarea Philippi, a journey of two days. This town lay at the foot of the snow-capped Mount Hermon. (It is here where the most eastern source of the river Jordan is found, gushing out from a cave. It is a very beautiful area.) Jesus and the disciples spent a few days in this place, away from the hostility of the Pharisees. Jesus took this opportunity to talk to his disciples, and started by asking them who men thought he was, then who did they think he was. It was at this point that Peter made his famous confession, "You are the Christ, the Son of the Living God" (Matthew 16:16). Jesus replied, "And I tell you that you are Peter, and on this rock I will build my church, and the gates of Hades will not overcome it"

(Matthew 16:18). The rock is the statement that Peter made ("You are the Christ..."), and not Peter himself.

Then the Lord started to prepare the disciples for the fact that he was going to suffer, die and rise again. They did not want to hear this, and Peter spoke out. The Lord turned to Peter and rebuked him. "Get behind me Satan!" he said (Matthew 16:23). Peter could be so wrong at times, but sometimes he was so right. Jesus then gave a hint of the event, which was shortly to follow, the Transfiguration. "Some who are standing here will not taste of death before they see the Son of Man coming in his kingdom" (Matthew 16:28). The time spent in this place was probably about a week. A suggestion has been made that Peter's great confession was made on the Sabbath, and then there were six days in between when the Lord no doubt taught his disciples more of his forthcoming death. Then, the following Sabbath evening, Jesus took his three closest disciples (Peter, James and John) up Mount Hermon to pray. The eight days, which are mentioned in Luke 9:28, must be these six days plus the two Sabbath days.

They spent time in prayer, and as Jesus was praying, he was transfigured before the disciples. His face and clothes shone brightly, and Moses and Elijah appeared and talked to the Lord about his approaching death in Jerusalem. The three disciples had been sleeping, but were now awake, and knew it was Moses and Elijah with Jesus. Peter spoke up, wanting to prolong the scene, by erecting three tents for Jesus and his visitors. It was all he could think of to say. He was overcome with the wonder of what he was seeing, but also afraid. A cloud then came down and engulfed them all and a voice came out from it, saying, "This is my Son, whom I love; ...Listen to him!" (Matthew 17:5). The disciples had to realise that Jesus was

CHAPTER THREE

not the same as Moses and Elijah. He was very special, indeed unique; he was God's Son. Then Jesus was alone again. The disciples had fallen down in fear, so Jesus went over to them and touched them, saying, "Get up. Don't be afraid" (Matthew 17:7). This scene was the high point of the Lord's time on earth. They had been in the presence of God here and had seen the Lord glorified, giving them a glimpse of the Kingdom of God. It must have greatly strengthened both the Lord and the three disciples. From here onwards, it was literally downhill all the way, right up to his humiliation and death. Then they descended the mountain. Jesus told the disciples to keep what they had witnessed to themselves, until after "the Son of Man had risen from the dead" (Mark 9:9). However, the three disciples were not sure what the "rising from the dead" meant, and they discussed this further amongst themselves. What they did ask Jesus was what it meant when the scribes said that Elijah must come first. This was a quotation from Malachi 4:5-6. It refers to John the Baptist, coming before the Messiah, to restore all things. Jesus told them that, just as John had been killed, so he also would suffer and die. The disciples seemed to understand Jesus here.

By now, it was morning, and they had arrived at the bottom of the mountain, where the remaining nine disciples were. With them was a large crowd of people, and Jesus noticed that some scribes were there, questioning them. When the crowd saw Jesus, they ran to him eagerly. Jesus asked the scribes what was going on. One of the people there spoke up. This man had brought his only son for healing. The child was possessed by an evil spirit and was out of control. His father had asked the nine disciples to heal him, but they had not been able to. These were the disciples who had not been chosen to watch the

Transfiguration. They were still spiritually immature. This was why they had not been able to heal this boy. The Lord seemed disappointed in them. "O unbelieving generation, how long shall I stay with you? How long shall I put up with you? Bring the boy to me" (Mark 9:19). These words, which Jesus spoke, seem to be directed at the nine disciples in particular. Jesus, having established that his father believed in him, then healed the boy, by casting out the evil spirit. The nine disciples asked Jesus later, why they had not been able to do this. Jesus explained to them that their faith was not yet mature enough. If they started to pray consistently, their faith would grow, and they would reach spiritual maturity.

Chapter Four

Now it was time to leave this area, and head south, on a journey which would take the Lord to Jerusalem. They travelled through Galilee, trying not to attract any attention to themselves. On the way, Jesus talked again of his death and resurrection. It was important that the disciples realised that this was going to happen, but still they did not understand what he was saying, and were afraid to ask him. They disputed amongst themselves who would be the greatest in the Kingdom of Heaven [1]. Jesus knew that they were doing this, but did not say anything at the time. However, he did come back to this later on.

At some point on this journey, it would appear that John and the other disciples split up from Jesus and Peter, and met a man who was casting out devils in the name of Jesus. They asked him to join them, but the man would not, so they told him he should not therefore cast out devils any more.

Jesus and Peter had now arrived at Capernaum. In Israel at that time, every male aged twenty and over was expected to make an annual contribution to the temple treasury, preferably before, or if not, just after the Passover. Jesus had not paid this yet, and the tribute collectors had found

Jesus to demand this money. They asked Peter if Jesus was intending to pay. Peter immediately said that he was, and then entered the house where Jesus was. Maybe this was Peter's own house. Jesus knew what Peter had said, and explained to him in parabolic form that, as they really belonged to God's royal household, they were exempt from paying tribute to an earthly king. In order not to offend anyone, they would pay the tax, but as neither of them seemed to have any money, it was provided for them by a miracle. The Lord told Peter to go and catch a fish, and in its mouth, there would be a four-drachma coin, which would be enough to pay the tax for both of them.

When the rest of the disciples had arrived at the house and Peter had returned from paying the tribute money, Jesus asked the disciples what they had been disputing among themselves on the road to Capernaum. He knew, of course, that they had been arguing about who would be the greatest in the Kingdom of Heaven. This had probably been brought on by the fact that three of them had been chosen to go up the Mount of Transfiguration, and the rest were left behind. Perhaps those three thought that they were better than the others were, or the nine were feeling jealous. It was also a common Jewish view that there were different ranks in the Kingdom of Heaven.

Jesus sat down and began to deal with this question of who was the greatest. He called a little child to him. (Maybe this was one of Peter's children.) He explained that whoever was humble like this child would be great in the Kingdom of Heaven. A child's simple, trusting atti-

CHAPTER FOUR

tude was the right attitude. He also explained that God values children. These words no doubt pricked John's conscience, and he told Jesus about the incident on the way, when he had forbidden the man to cast out devils. Had he been right to do this? Jesus answered by saying "Whoever is not against us is for us" (Mark 9:40). He did not seem pleased with John's sectarian attitude. Then Peter asked a question about how many times he should forgive his brother. Perhaps he had recently fallen out with the other disciples. Jesus then spent time teaching his disciples about forgiveness and other related teaching. This can be found in Matthew 18, Mark 9:35-50, Luke 9:47-50 and Luke 17:1-7. Jesus then spent the rest of the summer in Galilee, as it was safer to do so, because the Jews sought to kill him.

It was now autumn and nearly time for the Feast of the Tabernacles. Many people were setting off on the journey to Jerusalem. Jesus' own brothers were among them, and they suggested that Jesus should go too, so everyone there could see him. Jesus said, "No", as it was not yet the right time, so his brothers left without him. Jesus remained in Galilee for a little longer.

When he was ready to go, Jesus "resolutely set out for Jerusalem" (Luke 9:51). He knew what lay ahead for him, suffering, humiliation and death, but still he went. Pilgrims travelling from Galilee to Jerusalem would normally travel through Perea on the east side of the Jordan. The Lord and the disciples did not take this route. They took the quieter route through Samaria on the west of the Jordan. At one village in Samaria, Jesus sent messengers ahead to say that he was coming, but the people there would not receive him. They did not want any Jews there. James and John were furious about this, and asked the Lord if they could bring fire down from heaven as Elijah once did, and destroy these people. The memory of seeing Elijah on the Mount of Transfiguration may have put this in their minds. Jesus rebuked the disciples. He had come to save lives, not destroy them. They moved on to another village.

Matthew 8:18 tells us that Jesus saw multitudes of people gathering round him, so he gave the order to leave Samaria, and go to the other side of the Jordan, and into Decapolis. Here, a scribe, who had possibly followed Jesus from Samaria, came up to Jesus and said, "Teacher, I will follow you wherever you go" (Matthew 8:19). Jesus reminded the man that he was homeless, and following him demanded making sacrifices. Another man was standing there and Jesus asked him to follow him. This man's father had just died, and he asked Jesus if he could bury him first. According to Jewish law, this process would have taken a few days, by which time Jesus would have left the area. Another man wanted to join Jesus and the disciples, but first he wanted to go back home and say goodbye to everyone there. The answers Jesus gave to these men may have been surprising as, basically, he told them to leave these matters and follow him immediately. This was to show that following Jesus was more important than family ties or Jewish law. Jesus left people in no doubt about the hardships of following him. Some, who were half hearted, would be put off, but many became his disciples. Shortly after this, the Lord appointed seventy of them to go out in pairs before him, telling the people that Jesus would soon be coming to their town. Jesus gave them some advice similar to that which he had given the twelve disciples, when he had sent them out on missionary journeys. The seventy set off, and Jesus followed later, passing through these towns in Perea and Judea, on his way to Jerusalem. When the seventy reported back to

CHAPTER FOUR

Jesus, it was with great joy. They had been truly blessed in their work and Jesus rejoiced with them. It was here that a lawyer asked Jesus what he had to do to inherit eternal life. Jesus told him to do everything that was written in the law, to love God, and his neighbour as himself. The man asked, "Who is my neighbour"? Jesus then told the parable of the Good Samaritan.

Before arriving at Jerusalem, Jesus stopped at Bethany, a village just a few miles south east of the city. There is no mention of the twelve disciples here, so they must have gone straight to Jerusalem for the Feast of the Tabernacles. At Bethany, we meet for the first time Martha and Mary. Perhaps when the seventy had gone out to the towns, preparing the way for Jesus, Martha had told some of them to invite Jesus to stay with them. There is no mention of their brother Lazarus at this time, so he must have been in Jerusalem. According to Jewish law, they were required to construct a tent made from branches of trees. This was called a booth, and they were supposed to live in it over the festive period. It was to remind them of Israel's pilgrim days in the wilderness, and how God had blessed them with the harvest. (It was late September or early October.) This booth would be where the next events took place. Martha was the older sister, and she was very busy serving food to her guest. Mary, however, just sat at the feet of Jesus, listening to everything he said. Martha was annoyed about this, and asked Jesus to make her help with the work. His answer must have surprised Martha. Jesus told her gently that what she was doing was good, but what Mary had done was good too. The sisters were different, but Jesus loved them both, and their brother Lazarus (John 11:5). Their home became a special place to the Lord. It was a home where he was loved and respected, and he must have appreciated having a place to retire to from time to time.

The Feast of the Tabernacles lasted for seven days, but Jesus did not go up to Jerusalem until the middle of the Feast. He began to teach in the temple, and the Jews were amazed at what he had to say. They wondered how he could know so much, when he had not had a formal education. Jesus told them that this was God's teaching, and he was bringing it to them. Some people believed him, and others did not. He had caused quite a commotion in the temple, so the Pharisees and chief priests were not happy. Knowing their thoughts, Jesus told them that soon he would be going away, and they would not be able to find him. He was referring to his death and resurrection, but the Jews did not realise this.

The seventh and last day of the Feast was a special day, when Jews thought about the coming of the Messiah. Jesus was in the temple again on this day. A ritual pouring of water took place at this Feast, when water was taken from the pool of Siloam, and poured by the High Priest into a basin at the foot of the altar. Wine was also poured into the basin. This was a prayer to ask God for rain needed for their crops, and the ritual symbolised the outpouring of the Holy Spirit when the Messiah came. While this was happening, Jesus stood in the temple and cried, saying, "If anyone is thirsty, let him come to me and drink" (John 7:37). He was saying that he was the Messiah they were looking for, but the people were divided in their opinion about Jesus. The Pharisees wanted to have Jesus arrested, but the temple officers would not touch him, as they had never heard anyone speak like this before. The Pharisees said that only the ignorant, unlearned people were deceived by the words of Jesus, not important or educated people. Nicodemus (who we met

CHAPTER FOUR

in John 3) was present, and he spoke up, even though it was in rather a timid way. "Does our law condemn a man without first hearing him to find out what he is doing?" (John 7:51). The Pharisees answered by saying that no prophet would come out of Galilee, and Nicodemus did not say any more. After this, the people dispersed.

The next day was called the Octave (the eighth day), and worshippers gathered in the temple again. The scribes and Pharisees had brought to Jesus a woman accused of adultery. They were hoping to catch him out. They must have wondered what he was going to do with her, and hoped that whatever it was would give them grounds to accuse him. The law stated that such a person should be stoned. Jesus knew what to do. He wrote something on the ground, and said, "If any one of you is without sin, let him be the first to throw a stone at her" (John 8:7). The scribes and Pharisees were challenged. Jesus had reached their consciences with his words, and, one by one, they left the temple. Jesus remained alone with the woman. He told her that he did not condemn her, but not to sin any more.

During the Feast, the temple had been illuminated with candles and torches. Now Jesus spoke again, and proclaimed, "I am the light of the world" (John 8:12). He taught the scribes and Pharisees, and then the Jews. Some of the Jews believed him, but others took up stones to throw at Jesus, and drive him out of the temple. However, Jesus hid for a while, and then managed to walk away safely.

The next day was the Sabbath. Jesus was walking somewhere near the temple with his disciples, when he noticed a blind man. The recent contact with the Pharisees had influenced the disciples, and they went along with the idea that a man's affliction was a direct punishment for sin. If the person was (in this case) blind from birth, then it was his parents' sin, which was being punished. Jesus told them that the purpose of the man's blind condition was rather to show everyone the works of God. Since Adam, sin and sickness have come into the world, and God allows it, but has the power to heal if he desires to. The previous day, Jesus had told the people that he was the light of the world, and today, he referred to this again, then, healed the blind man, by anointing his eyes and telling him to wash in the pool of Siloam. This healing caused quite a commotion amongst the people and the Pharisees, especially as it was the Sabbath day. Some did not believe the man had been blind at all, so they found his parents and asked them. The couple confirmed that their son had indeed been born blind, but as they were afraid of the Pharisees, they told them to ask their son himself who it was who had restored his sight. The young man said that all he knew was that he was blind, but now he could see. He was sure the man who had healed him was from God, or else how could he do such a marvellous thing? The Pharisees cast him out of the temple for saying this, but Jesus heard about it and went to find him. He told him who he was, and the man worshipped him.

Some of the Pharisees had remained with Jesus, and he spoke to them again. He told them that he was the Good Shepherd (John 10), and he was soon to lay down his life for his sheep. The Pharisees were unable to understand this allegory, as they were spiritually blind. The word "parable" in some versions of John 10:6 means an allegory or illustration, rather than a parable like the ones we find in the other Gospels. Some of the Jews understood the Lord, but some did not. Yet again, there was a division amongst them.

Jesus then left Jerusalem to begin his ministry in Perea. He would return briefly for the Feast of Dedication in December, about three months later, then spend another three months in Perea, before returning to Jerusalem the week before his last Passover. The Perean Ministry contains a lot of teaching and parables. Luke chapters 11 to 17 record the details, and John's Gospel contains many incidents, which took place in Jerusalem. Some of the teaching was similar to what had been taught in Galilee, but this time it was more advanced.

Jesus and the disciples left Jerusalem for Perea. On the way, Jesus stopped to pray in a certain place. This might have been the locality where John the Baptist had been, and therefore prompted the response the disciples made, when they said, "Lord teach us to pray, just as John taught his disciples" (Luke 11:1). The Lord then told them the "Lord's Prayer" again, as he had done at the Sermon on the Mount.

The events recorded in Luke 11-17, are probably in chronological order. Matthew 12:22-45 appears to be another account of the first incident we read about in Luke 11, the healing of a demonised dumb and blind man. There were Pharisees present, and they attributed this power to Satan. Others asked for a sign from heaven to show that Jesus was from God. Jesus addressed the Pharisees and exposed them for what they were. In the past Israel had been guilty of idolatry, but now they were in a much worse state. They were self-righteous, blasphemers and hypocrites. As he was speaking, a woman cried out, extolling the blessedness of the mother of Jesus. Jesus did not welcome this sort of praise, as it detracted from his work on earth as the Saviour. "Blessed rather are those that hear the word of God and obey it" (Luke 11:28), he replied.

One Pharisee who was there asked Jesus to dine with him [2]. Jesus accepted the invitation, but surprised his host by not washing before the meal. The ceremonial washing before a meal was an important Jewish ritual, but Jesus had ignored it. He did this to show those present (Pharisees and teachers of the law) that they paid more attention to the outside of their bodies than the inside. They stuck to the letter of the law on some matters, but inside they were wicked. The Pharisees hoped that Jesus would say something, which they could use to accuse him, and deliberately tried to provoke him. By now many people had gathered at the scene. Jesus then addressed his disciples, warning them about the yeast (false teaching) of the Pharisees. Most of them were just hypocrites, but if they could fool the people, they could not fool God, so the disciples were not to fear them. God would look after them, so there was no need to worry. Jesus then used a parable to illustrate that it was foolish to think only about this life, while neglecting God. This was the parable of the foolish rich man. There are 13 parables in the Perean Ministry. They were easily understood by everyone, and were evangelical. They were as follows:

The good Samaritan ....Luke 10:25-37

The good friend..Luke 11:5-13

The rich fool...Luke 12:13-21

The barren fig tree.......................................Luke 13:6-9

The great banquet..Luke 14:15-24

The lost sheep...Luke 15:1-7

CHAPTER FOUR

The lost coin...Luke 15:8-10

The lost son..Luke 15:11-32

The shrewd manager...................................Luke 16:1-13

The rich man and Lazarus ....Luke 16:19-31

The persistent widow....................................Luke 18:1-8

The Pharisee and the tax collector ....Luke 18:9-14

The unmerciful servant........................Matthew 18:23-35

Jesus then continued to address his Perean disciples, and encouraged them to work hard, and to be ready for the time when he would return to them. He warned them that the times ahead would not be easy. Then he addressed the crowds who had gathered, and explained that people would be divided because of him.

Not long after this, Jesus was told about an incident which had taken place, possibly some time ago. Some

Galileans were offering sacrifices in the temple, when Pilate ordered them to be killed. Jesus knew what the people were thinking. They thought that these Galileans must have sinned badly to suffer such a fate. This was not the case, and Jesus reminded them of another unfortunate incident which had taken place. The tower at the pool of Siloam had fallen and killed eighteen people. That had not been a matter of punishment either. The whole Jewish nation was guilty, and they all needed to repent and accept Jesus, or they would die. To explain this further, he then went on to tell them the parable of the barren fig tree (Luke 13:6-9).

The next recorded incident is of another healing on a Sabbath day, which resulted in another controversy between Jesus and the Jewish authorities. This time the Lord was in one of the synagogues of Perea, when he noticed a woman who had been suffering for eighteen years with a condition which meant she could not straighten herself up, probably osteoporosis. This woman was a believer, but still in bondage to Satan, so she could not look at the Lord's face. She was morally and physically infirm. Jesus healed her and helped her to straighten up. She glorified God, but the ruler of the synagogue complained to the people that Jesus should not have healed her on the Sabbath day. Jesus said that this attitude was hypocritical. They all looked after their animals well on the Sabbath day, so why could he not help this woman when she needed it. The incident gave the people another picture of the wretched state that Israel was in at this time. Looking to Jesus would bring complete healing. Eventually the people were ashamed at their attitude, and rejoiced at what Jesus had done. Jesus then repeated the parables of the mustard seed and the yeast, which he had

CHAPTER FOUR

told in Galilee, in order to give these people further teaching on the Kingdom of God.

By now, it was December, and Jesus went to Jerusalem for the Feast of Dedication [3]. This feast lasted for eight days. He was walking in the temple, in Solomon's porch, and the Jews soon gathered round him, asking if he really was the Christ or not. Jesus replied that he had already told them that he was indeed the Christ, but they had not believed him. Even witnessing the miracles had not convinced them, because they were not his sheep. Jesus said, "My sheep listen to my voice; I know them, and they follow me" (John 10:27). He also said that he and the Father are one, which the Jews thought was blasphemy, so, they tried to stone him, but Jesus got away from them safely.

Chapter Five

Jesus went back over the Jordan, to carry on his ministry in Perea. He began at the place where John the Baptist had first baptised. It is difficult to be certain about the exact order of events in the second half of the Perean ministry, but we do know that Jesus taught in many cities and villages. He spoke to Pharisees, scribes, publicans and the ordinary people, teaching them and telling them parables. At one point, some of the Pharisees came to Jesus, telling him to leave the area, or Herod would kill him, but he would not go. He told them to tell "that fox" that he was going to carry on his work. The Lord could not have been worried by the threat, as he knew his time to die had not yet come. On another occasion, he dined with a chief Pharisee on the Sabbath day and healed a man with dropsy (a condition where fluid accumulated in the body). Afterwards he told the parable of the great banquet.

While Jesus was in Perea, he was given a message that his good friend Lazarus from Bethany was sick. "This sickness will not end in death. No, it is for God's glory so that God's Son may be glorified through it," Jesus replied (John 11:4), and he sent the messenger back to Bethany. He stayed for a further two days where he was. Then he

CHAPTER FIVE

told the disciples that it was time to go to Judea, but they were worried. They remembered that only a short time ago, at the Feast of Dedication, the Jews had tried to stone Jesus. They did not want him to go back anywhere near Jerusalem. Jesus then told them that Lazarus was dead, but he was going to wake him. The disciple Thomas then said, "Let us also go, that we may die with him" (John 11:16). He could see that Jesus had made his mind up to go to Bethany, and they would not be able to stop him. They may as well go with him, he thought, even if it meant they would die at the hands of the Jews. Such was Thomas's commitment to the Lord at this stage.

The journey to Bethany would have taken about a day, and when they arrived there, Martha came out to meet them. She was very upset because Lazarus had died; in fact, he had been in the grave for four days already. One suggestion for the order of events is as follows. The messenger left Bethany on the Sunday, and reached Jesus on the Monday, by which time Lazarus had died. He would have been buried on the Monday, as the custom was to bury the dead on the same day as their death. Jesus stayed in Perea for a further two days, until the Wednesday, and then travelled the day's journey to Bethany, arriving on the Thursday. Lazarus was raised on this day, then, Jesus spent the Friday and the Saturday with the family at Bethany, and returned to Perea and Ephraim on the Sunday.

Lazarus had been a well-known, respected Jew; so many people were upset about his death. Many Jews came from nearby Jerusalem to comfort the sisters. Martha could not help herself saying, "Lord, if you had been here, my brother would not have died" (John 11:21). She could not understand why Jesus had not come to them earlier. She had the faith to believe that Jesus could have saved him;

in fact, she believed that he could do anything. Jesus told her that her brother would rise again, but Martha thought he was talking about the resurrection at the last day. She must have had no idea of what Jesus was going to do. The Lord then asked to see Mary, so Martha went to get her. As Mary left the house, the Jews that were with her, followed, thinking she was going to the grave of Lazarus, When she saw Jesus, Mary fell at his feet, weeping, and said to him the same thing that Martha had said, that if Jesus had been there, Lazarus would not have died. She had great faith too. The Jews were also weeping, and the Lord was "deeply moved in spirit and troubled" (John 11:33). He could feel the sorrow that death brought to the world, and he wept. Then Jesus asked to see the grave, which was in a cave. Well-to-do people such as Lazarus, were buried in private tombs in caves, and often in gardens. Jesus asked for the stone to be removed from the entrance to the cave. Martha reminded him that Lazarus had now been dead for four days. It was a common Jewish idea that a dead body would begin to corrupt on the fourth day. Jesus gently reminded her that she was about to see the glory of God, as he had said in his original message to them four days ago. When the stone had been removed from the cave, Jesus prayed, then, called for Lazarus to come out of the grave.

Jesus had told Martha that he was the "resurrection and the life" (John 11:25), and this proved it. Lazarus came walking out, still in his grave clothes, but alive. Many of the Jews believed in Jesus this day, but others went straight to the Pharisees in Jerusalem to tell them all about what had just happened. They called a meeting, probably on the Friday, with the chief priests, to decide what to do with Jesus. There was no doubt that he had performed this miracle, and others, so the authorities were worried

CHAPTER FIVE

that everyone would believe on him. They thought that Jesus would lead a Jewish rebellion against the Romans, and all the Jews would perish. They did not want that. The high priest, Caiaphas, thought that it would be better if one man died, rather than a whole nation, so they agreed to have Jesus put to death. In fact, Caiaphas, as high priest, prophesied that Jesus should die for the nation, and in so doing, gather together the children of God that were scattered abroad. This was the last prophecy made in Israel. Someone, perhaps Nicodemus must have warned Jesus about these plans. As it was not safe for the Lord to stay near Jerusalem, he went to Perea with his disciples, to a city called Ephraim.

The exact location of this city is not clear, but after spending some time here with his disciples, Jesus travelled north, as far as the borders of Samaria and Galilee (Luke 17:11). We know from Mark 15:41, that many Galilean women accompanied Jesus on his last journey to Jerusalem, so he must have met up with them at this time. It is unlikely that these women had been travelling with Jesus since his last visit to Galilee in the autumn. So, having met up with all those who were to accompany him on his journey, the Lord then travelled south. This group of believers must have given the Lord some encouragement on his final journey to Jerusalem. As they journeyed, many other people joined them, and Jesus healed the sick, and taught. We are told of a few incidents in more detail, the first one being the healing of ten lepers.

Jesus and his followers had arrived at a certain village, when they saw in the distance, ten lepers. These men cried out to Jesus to have mercy on them. They wanted him to heal them. Jesus did not approach them or heal them immediately, but simply told them to go and show themselves to the priests. This was so that they could be declared clean. The lepers obeyed in faith and, on the way to the priests, they were all cleansed of their leprosy. Nine of the men carried on to the priests, but one man came back to Jesus immediately. He went right up to him, and fell at his feet, thanking Jesus for what he had done for him. He was singled out as a Samaritan, so presumably, the other nine were Jews, but they had not bothered to thank the Lord, or give glory to God. The Samaritan showed that his faith was real, and he was cleansed both in body and spirit. The nine Jews were healed in body only. It was a shame that they had the faith to come to Jesus for healing, but did not want to follow him as Lord.

The Pharisees still came to Jesus with their questions, trying to catch him out. They wanted to know about divorce, and when the Kingdom of God would come. They tried to catch him out, but Jesus could always answer them. When the Pharisees had left, Jesus and his followers moved to someone's house. Here, the disciples asked him to say some more about divorce. They were not quite clear about it yet. It was not long before the news got round that Jesus was in the area. A group of parents came to see Jesus, bringing their young children with them. They wanted Jesus to lay his hands on them and pray for them. The disciples tried to stop them. Jesus had had a busy day, answering question after question, and they thought he would not want to be bothered with little children. How wrong they were! Jesus was indignant, and called the children to him. He took them up in his arms and blessed them. "Let the little children come to me, and do not hinder them, for the Kingdom of God

CHAPTER FIVE

belongs to such as these" he said (Luke 18:16). Jesus had to remind the disciples that young children were included in the Kingdom of God, and he was always happy to make time for them.

Jesus and his followers left this area, and headed towards Jerusalem. As they were going along, a young man, described as a ruler, came running up to Jesus, and knelt down. "Good teacher, what must I do to inherit eternal life?" he asked him (Luke 18:18). Jesus told him that only God was good. Did he really think that Jesus was God? Was he prepared to sell all his possessions and give the money to the poor? He was a rich man and, although a good man, he was not prepared to leave everything and follow Jesus, and he went away sad. Jesus was sad too, and he told the disciples that it was hard for a rich man to enter into the Kingdom of God. Peter reminded the Lord that he and the other disciples had left all that they had to follow him. Jesus answered by saying that he would make it up to them. Anyone who left everything to follow him, would receive back much more than they had left behind, both in this life and the next. He told the twelve disciples that they would each have their own throne in his Kingdom. He also said that the first shall be last; and the last shall be first.

At some point on the way to Jerusalem, Jesus took the twelve disciples to one side, to talk to them on their own. He reminded them that he was soon going to be betrayed and crucified, but he would rise again. The Lord must have felt that the disciples needed to hear this again. They had not really taken this in yet; in fact, it was not until after the resurrection that they really understood.

After this, Salome, the mother of James and John, and Jesus' aunt, came to Jesus to ask him a favour. Presumably, she was one of the women who had come down from Galilee with Jesus. James and John were with her, as she asked Jesus to allow her sons to sit either side of him in his Kingdom. She wanted them to have the highest honour, and so did they. The Lord gently explained to them that they did not realise what they were asking. To earn such an honour would demand the greatest suffering first, as glory only comes after suffering. Were they really prepared for that? In any case, it was not for the Lord to decide these things, but God the Father. The other disciples were very annoyed with James and John for asking this, but Jesus told them that if anyone desired to be great amongst them, let him take the lowest place, and be as a servant to the others. This was true greatness in the Kingdom of God.

The Perean ministry was now finished and Jesus and his followers crossed the river Jordan, and arrived at Jericho. Jericho was only about fifteen miles from Jerusalem, and was an important, prosperous city at this time, as it lay on the caravan route from Arabia to Damascus. It had a mild climate, so at this time of year (early spring), it would feel more like summer. Jericho was also called the City of Palms, as palm trees surrounded it. The Jericho of the Old Testament was actually in a different place. That town was burned down and destroyed, but was later rebuilt a few miles away. These two sites may explain the apparent difficulties with the account of the healing of the blind men in Matthew 20, Mark 10 and Luke 18. Jesus was well known now and, as he passed through Jericho, a large crowd soon gathered. Many people wanted to see him, even if it was just out of curiosity.

One of these people was Zacchaeus, a chief publican or tax collector in the town. He was a rich man, but unfortunately for him, he was not very tall, and he could not

CHAPTER FIVE

see anything of Jesus at all, because of the crowd. As he really did want to see him, Zacchaeus ran ahead and climbed up a sycamore tree, so that when Jesus passed by, he would have a good view. When Jesus did pass by, he stopped and looked directly at him, and told him to come down, as he wanted to stay at his house. Zacchaeus was overjoyed, and quickly climbed down the tree. The people in the crowd were not happy, because they knew that Zacchaeus was a dishonest man, as many of the tax collectors were. They all hated him, and could not understand why Jesus had chosen to go to his house. Zacchaeus knew that he was a sinner too, and it was not long before he admitted to the Lord that he had cheated people out of their money, but he would pay them back, four times as much. He would also give half of his possessions to the poor. He was truly repentant, and Jesus knew it. "Today salvation has come to this house", he said (Luke 19:9). It was a lesson to everyone that Jesus had come to seek out the lost, the sinners and the unloved in the world.

The next morning, the journey to Jerusalem was resumed, but, before long, another incident took place. The assumption is made that the accounts in Matthew 20, Mark 10, and Luke 18 refer to one incident, which took place near Jericho. Two blind men were sat begging by the road, which led out of Jericho. A crowd had followed Jesus, and the blind men heard that it was Jesus who was passing by. One of them, called Bartimaeus, spoke out. "Lord, Son of David have mercy on us!" he cried (Matthew 20:30). The crowd tried to quieten him, but Jesus stopped and called them to him. Someone took them to Jesus, who asked them what they wanted him to do for them. Their answer was that they wanted to be able to see. Jesus was touched by their faith and healed them immediately. The men then followed Jesus with the others and praised God. As they continued on their way to Jerusalem, Jesus told the people with him the parable of the Ten Minas (Luke 19:11-28).

Chapter Six

The Passover was now only a few days away, and many people were wondering if Jesus would come to Jerusalem or not. The chief priests and Pharisees had ordered that if anyone knew where Jesus was, they should let them know. Meanwhile, Jesus had arrived in Bethany, the place where Lazarus, Martha and Mary lived. It was Friday, six days before the Passover. The next day, the Sabbath, Jesus and the disciples were invited for a meal at the home of Simon the Leper. Lazarus, Martha and Mary were also invited, Martha was helping to serve the food, and Lazarus was sat at the table with Jesus. Mary had brought with her an alabaster box of precious ointment. It would have been worth a lot of money. Because she was so spiritual, she understood that Jesus was about to die, and she decided that now was the time to use the ointment. She was anointing his body in preparation for his burial. The Lord was so pleased with her devotion and understanding, but he rebuked the others when they criticised her. No one else had thought of doing this. Judas was particularly annoyed, and said that she would have been better to sell the ointment and give the money to the poor. He did not really care for the poor; it was all pretence, as was his discipleship.

Many people heard that Jesus was in Bethany, and went over to see him and Lazarus too. They had heard that Jesus had brought this man back to life again, and they wanted to see them both. The chief priests even contemplated putting Lazarus to death, as he was such a witness to the power of God and many Jews were believing in Jesus as a result.

The next day, Sunday (John 12:12), Jesus left Bethany and headed west, towards the Mount of Olives and Jerusalem, a journey of two miles. It was time to make his entry into Jerusalem as King of the Jews. This would fulfil the prophecy made by Zechariah that the king would come unto them humbly, riding upon an ass's colt (Zechariah 9:9). About half way there, near a village called Bethpage, Jesus sent two disciples to collect an ass's colt that he knew would be there. He told them to untie it, and if anyone stopped them, to say that the Lord needed it. The disciples returned with the colt, which had never been ridden before, and put their coats on it. The city was full of people who had come for the Passover week, and a large crowd had gathered in anticipation of Jesus' arrival.

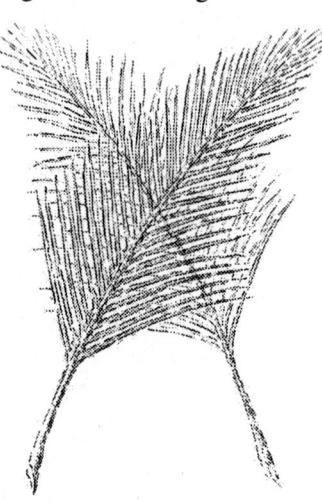

Many of them went out to meet him, as he descended the Mount of Olives. They had cut down palm branches, and when they saw Jesus approaching, riding on the colt, they placed them on the ground, along with their coats. This was the way they greeted royalty in those days. Today we would put down a red carpet. They rejoiced and

CHAPTER SIX

praised God, saying, "Blessed is the king who comes in the name of the Lord!" (Luke 19:38). Eventually, everyone was joining in, including the twelve disciples, although they did not understand the significance of the royal entry into Jerusalem, until after the resurrection. Some people had come because they had heard about the raising of Lazarus, and they were now able to talk to those who had been eyewitnesses. The Pharisees were also there, and they did not like what they saw. They wanted Jesus to rebuke his disciples, but he answered them by saying that if he silenced them, the stones on the ground would cry out. This was a phrase, which was sometimes used by the Jews when a sin was committed.

The procession carried on, and soon had their first glimpse of Jerusalem. Jesus could not help but weep when he saw the city, as he knew the future. He would be rejected there, and the city would eventually be destroyed. More and more people came to see what was going on, and who was there. "This is Jesus, the prophet from Nazareth in Galilee," they were told by the multitude (Matthew 21:11). Jesus went to the temple and looked around, but he did not say anything. This was the day when the Jews selected their Passover lamb, and today, Jesus had not only presented himself to the Jews as their King, but also as the True Passover Lamb. When evening was approaching, Jesus and the twelve disciples returned to Bethany, where they were lodging.

Early the next morning, they returned to Jerusalem. On the way, Jesus noticed a fig tree in the distance and, as he was hungry, he decided to stop there and pick some figs to eat. Although it was early spring, the tree may have had some of last year's crop on it, or the new crop may have started to grow already. However, when the Lord reached the tree, there was no fruit at all, only leaves. The leaves gave the impression that the tree would be fruitful, but on closer examination, it was found to be barren. This false hope exactly illustrated the condition of Israel at that time, and so Jesus cursed the tree, so that no fruit would ever grow on it again. The disciples heard all this, but it is doubtful whether they understood the significance on that day, even though Jesus had already told them the parable of the fig tree a few months earlier.

They continued walking, and soon reached the temple at Jerusalem. Jesus was again furious about the thieves and swindlers who gathered there. He also noticed that some people were using the temple as a short cut from one part of the city to another, so he drove the offenders out as he had done so at the beginning of his ministry. When the temple was a fit place for worship again, Jesus began to teach, and the people listened well, as they were amazed at his words. He also healed the sick people who came to him. The children in the temple began to shout, "Hosanna to the Son of David", as they had heard the people shout the previous day (Matthew 21:15). The chief priests and scribes were not pleased, but Jesus said, "From the lips of children and infants you have ordained praise" (Matthew 21:16). Jesus spent the day in Jerusalem, then went back to Bethany in the evening.

The next day was Tuesday, and was the Lord's last working day. It turned out to be a very full day, and putting events into chronological order is not easy. It began early, with the walk from Bethany to Jerusalem. They passed by the fig tree, which Jesus had cursed the day before, and which was now dried up, from the roots. Peter noticed this and pointed it out to the others. He could see the miracle, but the Lord wanted him to understand the meaning of it. "Have faith in God", he said to the disciples (Mark 11:22). The lesson he was trying to teach them

CHAPTER SIX

was that Israel lacked simple faith, so they were barren like this fig tree, but the disciples need not be like that. With faith, they would be able to do anything, even cast mountains into the sea. "Whatever you ask for in prayer, believe that you have received it, and it will be yours" (Mark 11:24). Faith gave power to prayer, but a forgiving attitude was also required. The Lord reminded the disciples that they should not harbour grudges against their brethren.

They continued on their way, and soon arrived in Jerusalem, and entered the temple. Jesus began to teach once again, but the authorities, which had been afraid to interfere the day before, were now ready to challenge him. They wanted to know who gave him authority to teach in the temple. The Lord knew how to deal with them, and answered them with a question. "John's baptism—was it from heaven, or from men? Tell me!" (Mark 11:30). They did not know how to answer him. They dared not say anything against John, as the people regarded John as a prophet, and the authorities feared the people. They did not want to say that John had baptised with heavenly authority, as they had not believed that. As they could not give an answer, the Lord would not discuss the matter further, but carried on with his teaching.

He told the people some new parables; this was the third series of parables, and they spoke of judgement, and the end times. They were as follows:

The workers in the vineyard .... Matthew 20:1-16

The two sons .... Matthew 21:28-32

The tenants .... Matthew 21, Mark 12, Luke 20

The wedding banquet .... Matthew 22:1-14

These parables pronounced judgement on the chief priests and Pharisees, and they knew it. Later in the day, the Lord told two more parables to the twelve disciples.

The ten virgins ....Matthew 25:1-13

The talents................................Matthew 25:14-30

The parable of the ten minas (pounds) in Luke 19:11-27 also belongs with this series, but this had probably been told after the conversion of Zacchaeus. This makes a total of seven in all.

The chief priests and Pharisees then met together to discuss how they might entangle the Lord as he spoke. They decided to send spies to him, with what was supposed to be an innocent question. "Is it right for us to pay taxes to Caesar, or not?" (Luke 20:22). Some of these spies were younger Pharisees, and some were Herodians. The Herodians were a political party at that time, in contrast to the Pharisees, who were an ecclesiastical party. Some people thought that to pay tribute money to Caesar, was virtually saying that he was Israel's king, and this would be disloyal to God. If Jesus had answered no, do not pay Caesar, this might have caused a rebellion against the Romans. If Jesus had said yes, do pay, then it might have led the people to think that Jesus was not King of the Jews at all. Answering either yes or no, would have resulted in Jesus being in trouble with either the Romans, or the people. The Lord could see their motives, and was not going to fall into the trap they had set. He asked them to show him a coin. It had Caesar's imprint on it. "Then give to Caesar what is Caesar's, and to God what is God's," he said (Luke 20:25). The Lord had answered them perfectly, and they were amazed at his answer. They did not know what to say to him, so they left him alone.

CHAPTER SIX

The next group of people to question the Lord was a group of Sadducees, who came to ask him about the subject of resurrection and marriage. Like the Pharisees and Herodians, their motives were not genuine. The Sadducees didn't even believe in the resurrection. They intended to give the Lord a question he could not answer. He could and did answer them, trying to explain to them about resurrection, and the fact that there would be no need for marriage in Heaven. The Sadducees did not know what to say, and dared not ask him anything else, but a scribe had overheard this conversation, and had been impressed with the Lord's answer. He consulted with the Pharisees, and they came up with another insidious question for the Lord to deal with. "Teacher, which is the greatest commandment in the Law?" they asked him (Matthew 22:36). Jesus explained to them that to love the Lord God was the most important thing, and secondly to love your neighbour as you would love yourself. This covered everything, so no other commandments were necessary. The scribe was again impressed with the Lord's answer, but whether or not he became a believer, we do not know.

Jesus carried on teaching. He spoke directly to the Pharisees and scribes, exposing their hypocrisy, and warning the people of their wicked ways. At some stage, he must have been in the part of the temple where women were allowed. He was watching the people coming and going, when he noticed a poor widow putting two mites (what we would call coppers), into the treasury. All around her were rich men, casting their gifts into the treasury. The Lord did not speak to her, but pointed her out to the disciples, comparing her with the rich men. She had given so much more to God, as she had given all she had; she had not even kept one of the mites for herself.

The rich men, however, had only given a fraction of what they possessed. This incident serves as an important lesson to us all, that God notices the sacrifices we make for him.

At some point in the day, some Greeks (who had converted to Judaism) were worshipping in the temple. They desired to see Jesus, but did not like to go up to him directly. They asked the disciple Philip if they could see Jesus. Perhaps they knew Philip, or perhaps there was a family connection. (Philip is a Greek name.) He was not sure, so asked Andrew, his friend and fellow disciple, and the two men went to Jesus together with the request. We are not told specifically, but we presume that their request was granted, and Jesus spoke to them and the disciples of his forthcoming death. This was more or less the close of the Lord's public ministry. He was aware of the horror to come, but said, "Father glorify your name!" (John 12:28). A voice from heaven was heard, saying, "I have glorified it, and will glorify it again" (John 12:28). God had spoken audibly, as he had at the Lord's baptism, at the very start of his public ministry. It must have been an encouragement to hear his Father's voice at this time.

Before leaving the temple, Jesus said, "O Jerusalem, Jerusalem, you who kill the prophets, and stone those sent to you, how often I have longed to gather your children together, as a hen gathers her chicks under her wings, but you were not willing. Look, your house is left to you desolate" (Matthew 23:37-38). Here, Jesus was predicting the destruction of the temple, which would take place in AD 70. After this, Jesus left the temple, and withdrew from the crowds. The people were left to think about what he had said that day, and sadly, some of the rulers believed him, but did not confess him as their Lord, as they were afraid they might lose their positions of impor-

CHAPTER SIX

tance in the synagogue. Position and the praise of men meant more to them than the praise of God.

Jesus and the twelve disciples crossed over the brook Cedron (also called Kidron), and began to climb the Mount of Olives. Looking back at the temple they had just left, the disciples could not help admiring its beauty. Jesus reminded them that it was going to be destroyed, but they could hardly believe it. They carried on walking, then stopped for a rest. Peter, James, John and Andrew wanted to know more about the destruction of the temple, and what was going to happen in the future, so the Lord began a prophetic discourse, which can be found in Matthew 24, Mark 13 and Luke 21. It was here that Jesus told the disciples the parables of the ten virgins, and the talents, which both speak of the Lord's return. It was now evening, and the Lord and the twelve disciples spent the night somewhere on the Mount of Olives.

Chapter Seven

There were only two days left until the Passover supper (Wednesday and Thursday). The supper would be on the Thursday evening, so the Jews counted this as two days (Matthew 26:2). At that time a Jewish day was from sunset to sunset, so the evening was the beginning of a new day. Wednesday was spent quietly, away from the city; there are no details, but it is likely that Jesus would have visited the home at Bethany where he was so welcome. It was his last chance to rest before the ordeal which lay before him. It was on this day that we read that Satan entered into Judas Iscariot (Luke 22:3), and he left the others and went back to Jerusalem, and to the palace of the High Priest. There he talked to the chief priests, scribes, elders, and the captains of the temple guards, about how he could betray Jesus. They were pleased Judas had come to them, as they were looking for a way to kill Jesus, but were not sure how to do it without there being an uproar among the people. They would not have wanted any trouble on a feast day. Judas asked them what they would give him for doing this, and they agreed on thirty pieces of silver, the price of a slave (Exodus 21:32). Money was important to Judas, and we know from John 12:6 that he was a thief.

CHAPTER SEVEN

The Feast of Unleavened Bread began at the start of the 14th day of the month, which we would call April, and this particular year, that happened to be a Wednesday evening. Preparations could then be made for the Passover supper, which would be eaten on the Thursday evening. The Jews would have probably stopped working at about midday on the Thursday, and swept their homes, getting rid of any yeast which was in the house. This symbolised the removal of anything evil from the house. The Passover lamb would have been killed on the Thursday afternoon and eaten that night (the start of the 15th day). It was on the Wednesday evening when the disciples came to Jesus to ask him where they were going to eat the Passover meal. Jesus may not have wanted Judas to know where the place was just yet, in case he betrayed him too soon. There were a few more things he wanted to say to the disciples and he needed a bit more time with them in order to do this, so Jesus sent only Peter and John to Jerusalem, with instructions to follow a man with a pitcher of water. He would go into a house, which happened to have a large upper room, already furnished, and they were to ask permission to use this room for the Passover meal. They were to say to the man that the Master wanted to keep the Passover at this house with his disciples. This suggests that this was the home of one or more of the Lord's followers. Some people think it was the home of John Mark (the author of Mark's gospel) and his parents. The two men obeyed him and went off to make the necessary preparations, then, when everything was ready, Jesus sat down with the twelve disciples to eat the Passover supper. "I have eagerly desired to eat this Passover with you before I suffer," he said (Luke 22:15).

```
              disciple
disciple   ┌──────────┐   disciple
           │          │
disciple   │          │   disciple
           │          │
disciple   │          │   disciple
           │          │
Judas      │          │   disciple
           │          │
Jesus      │          │   disciple
           │          │
John       └──────────┘   Peter
```

They sat reclining round the long table, probably in a horseshoe format as suggested in the diagram above. The table would have been low, and the seats more like couches, on which people reclined rather than sat, with their head nearest the table and their feet stretching back. Seating arrangements were important to Jews, and sadly, this led to a squabble amongst the disciples about which of them was the most important. It seems that Judas had managed to get what was regarded as the best seat, that is the seat to the left side of Jesus, who was the head of the company, and the others were not happy about this [1]. Jesus had a few words with them about humility, and Peter then seems to have deliberately chosen the lowest place, opposite John. The Passover meal consisted of roast lamb with bitter herbs (usually horseradish), unleavened bread and four cups of red wine. Part of the ritual was the ceremonial washing of hands, which happened twice during the meal. The first time, the head of the company washed his hands, the second time, everybody washed. Jesus not only washed his hands but began to wash the disciples' feet, possibly starting with Peter, as he was on the end. Peter was not happy about the Lord doing this, but Jesus insisted, and said to him, "Unless I wash you, you have no part with me" (John 13:8). The Lord wanted to show them true service and humility, a subject which they had just been talking about. The feet washing was also symbolic of the fact that although they were inwardly 'clean', their daily walk must be kept clean too. However, Jesus said that there was one person there who was not clean, and by this, he was referring to Judas. Nobody said anything after this, but allowed the Lord to finish the feet washing. When he had finished, Jesus said that he hoped they would follow his example and serve one another too.

They carried on with the meal, and Jesus, with much sorrow, told the disciples that one of them was going to betray him. They all began to ask him if it was going to be them, and Peter, sitting opposite John, beckoned to him, and quietly asked him to find out who the traitor would be. John asked Jesus who it was, and he answered, "It is the one to whom I will give this piece of bread when I have dipped it in the dish" (John 13:26), and he dipped the bread in the charoseth (a mixture of apples and nuts).

Judas was first to receive it because he had occupied the chief place at the table, so the other disciples may not have realised that the Lord was saying that Judas was the traitor. As he passed the bread, Judas said "Surely not I, Lord?" (Matthew 26:22). Jesus said that it was, but no one else seems to have heard. At this point, we read that Satan entered once again into Judas, and Jesus said to him, "What you are about to do, do quickly" (John 13:27). Judas left the room, and went outside into the night. None of the others realised what had happened; they thought Jesus had sent Judas out to do some business, as he was in charge of the money. With Judas out of the way, the Lord could institute what we call the "Lord's supper".

They carried on with the meal, and as they were eating, Jesus took some of the bread, blessed it, broke it up, and passed it to the disciples. "Take and eat; this is my body", he said (Matthew 26:26). Then he took one of the cups of wine, and when he had given thanks, he gave it to the disciples, and they all had a drink. Jesus said, "This is my blood of the covenant, which is poured out for many for the forgiveness of sins" (Matthew 26:28). He also said that he would not drink any more wine until the Kingdom of God had come. 1 Corinthians 11:23-26 gives us a little more information about this night, and explains that

CHAPTER SEVEN

when we eat the bread and drink the wine together, we are remembering the Lord's death.

When the supper was over, Jesus began to teach the eleven disciples. What he said is recorded in John chapters 14-17. He told them that he was going away to prepare a place for them in heaven, but God would send the Comforter, or Holy Spirit, to help them, so they need not be afraid. Then they sang a hymn and left the upper room. They were heading for the Mount of Olives. It is not clear where Jesus spoke his next discourse to them. It may have been in another room in the house, or it may have been as they were walking through the streets of Jerusalem. Jesus warned the disciples that they would have trouble in the world, and they may suffer persecution. Then he prayed for himself, that he might glorify God, and for the disciples, and for all believers.

It was probably just after this, that Jesus told Peter, "Simon, Simon, Satan has asked to sift you as wheat" (Luke 22:31). Peter was in danger, but the Lord said that he had been praying for him, and although he would fail him, it would only be temporary, and he wanted Peter to strengthen the others once his faith had been restored. "Lord, I am ready to go with you to prison and to death," Peter replied (Luke 22:33). Jesus predicted that Peter would deny him three times before the cock would crow twice in the morning, but Peter could not believe it, nor could the other disciples. Jesus told them that things were going to get difficult for them and they would have to be ready to face danger.

Then they crossed the brook Cedron, and walked to a small garden, called Gethsemane. They had been to this quiet little place before; perhaps it belonged to believers, who let the Lord go there to rest and pray. He was going to pray here now, and he told the disciples to sit down, except for Peter, James and John. Jesus took them with him further into the garden. These were the Lord's closest disciples; they were the ones who had witnessed the Transfiguration, and now they had the privilege of supporting the Lord in his last few hours before his arrest. He told them that he suddenly felt very sorrowful, but the three of them were to wait for him and watch, while he went further on to pray. "Father, if you are willing, take this cup from me; yet not my will, but yours be done," he prayed (Luke 22:42). It was a very difficult time for him, as the true horror of all that lay before him was now unfolding. His soul was in agony, and he was sweating profusely, as he who knew no sin was preparing to be made sin for us, but an angel came from heaven to strengthen him.

After praying for an hour, the Lord returned to the three disciples, but they had fallen asleep. "Could you not keep watch for one hour?" he said (Mark 14:37). He went to pray again, and when he returned to the disciples, they had fallen asleep again. This happened three times in all, so the disciples had not been much support to the Lord at all. The third time, Jesus told them to carry on sleeping. He was now composed after the time of prayer, and was ready to face his arrest. After a brief time of rest, Jesus told the three disciples to get up, and they joined the other disciples at the entrance of the garden. He told them that he was now going to be betrayed and, as he spoke, Judas was coming towards them with a large band of men. He had brought Roman soldiers, chief priests, scribes and elders. They were armed and some men were carrying torches and lanterns. Judas went up to Jesus and greeted him with a kiss. He had told the soldiers to arrest the person he would kiss, so this was their signal. Jesus approached the

CHAPTER SEVEN

band of men, and calmly asked them who they were looking for. "Jesus of Nazareth," they said, so he told them that he was the one they wanted. The men were taken by surprise because of the Lord's composure, and they were affected by his power. Some of them fell backwards. Jesus again told them that he was the man they wanted, so they should let the disciples go their way. Then they took Jesus, to arrest him. Peter could not cope with this and, as he was carrying a sword, he drew it and struck at one of the men, cutting off his right ear. This man was called Malchus, and he was a servant of the High Priest. Jesus told Peter to put his sword away. This was not the way things were going to be done, and in any case, if he wanted help, he could ask God to send him thousands of angels. Then he healed Malchus. The leaders bound Jesus as if he were a common thief, and led him away. The disciples fled, but one young man did try to follow Jesus.

Some people think this young man was John Mark. The suggestion is that Judas led the soldiers to the upper room, presuming that Jesus and the disciples would still be there. When he discovered that they had left, Judas rightly suspected that they would have gone on to the garden of Gethsemane, where they had been many times before. A young John Mark was asleep in the house, but the commotion had woken him up. He quickly grabbed a loose linen garment to wrap round himself and followed the band of men to Gethsemane. He hid, watching, and when

Jesus was led away, he tried to follow, but some of the men spotted him, and tried to seize him. However, he escaped from them, and they were left holding only his linen garment. The suggestion seems to make sense, as it is only Mark that tells us about the incident.

The Roman soldiers led Jesus away to the house of Annas, who was the father-in-law of the High Priest, and a former High Priest himself. He had been High Priest when the twelve-year-old Jesus questioned the Doctors of the Law in the temple. Perhaps Annas remembered that day. He must have retained some influence over the Jews, and he told them to take Jesus to Caiaphas the High Priest. By this time, Peter and John had returned to the scene, anxious to see what was happening to the Lord, but trying not to be noticed. John knew the High Priest, so he was allowed in his palace, but Peter remained outside until John asked the girl at the door to let Peter in also. John remained in the building, but Peter went over to a fire that was burning in the courtyard. At this time, large houses were often built in a quadrangular shape with an open courtyard or hall as it was sometimes called, in the middle. This would be where the fire was, and where Peter now stood with a group of officers and servants. Jesus was inside the house. The girl at the door had recognised Peter, and went over to him as he warmed himself by the fire. It was now the middle of the night, and he was cold. She asked him if he was one of Jesus' disciples, which he quickly denied. Peter then left the fire and walked to the porch, just as the cock crowed for the first time. Here he was questioned again, but denied for the second time that he had anything to do with Jesus.

Meanwhile, Caiaphas was questioning Jesus about his disciples and his doctrine. Jesus reminded him that he had spent the last few days speaking in the temple. If he

CHAPTER SEVEN

(Caiaphas) were to ask the people, they could tell him what he had said. One of the officers standing by did not like this answer, and struck Jesus with his hand. The Lord remained calm, but told them all that if he had said anything evil, they should prove it. Caiaphas called for the Jewish council, and although it was the middle of the night, they quickly came to the palace. They brought witnesses to speak out against Jesus, but they gave conflicting testimonies. Eventually, two men agreed that they had heard Jesus say that he would destroy the temple of God, but could build it up again in three days. They were remembering what Jesus had said to the Jews in the temple at the first Passover (John 2:19). "Destroy this temple, and I will raise it again in three days", was what he had actually said, referring to his own death. The Jews had not understood him at the time, and now they were twisting his words in order to accuse him. Jesus did not answer, so Caiaphas asked him if he was the Son of God, to which he replied that he was. Caiaphas considered this as blasphemous, and he tore his clothes in front of everybody. The Jews agreed that Jesus should be put to death; then they left to get some sleep. They would return in the morning. Jesus was left in the care of the guards and the servants, but they began to abuse him, spitting at him and pushing him. Some struck him with their hands, making fun of him.

Down in the courtyard, Peter was back at the fire. He had been hanging round the palace for about an hour now. One of the servants remembered seeing him in the garden of Gethsemane, when Jesus was arrested. He challenged Peter as to whether he was one of Jesus' followers. He could tell by his Galilean accent that he was not a local man. Peter began to curse and swear, and vehemently denied having anything to do with Jesus. Just then, the cock crowed for the second time, and Jesus who was in the room above, turned and looked at Peter. Peter saw the look, and remembered how the Lord had said he would deny him three times. He was bitterly ashamed, and left the house in tears.

In the morning (Friday) the Jewish council returned to the palace of Caiaphas. They had already decided Jesus was guilty, but now they had to agree on what to do with him next. They decided to bind him and take him to Pontius Pilate, as if he were a common criminal. Pilate was the Roman governor of Judea. As it was a feast day, the Jews did not want to be exposed to the heathen Romans in case they were 'defiled' by them, which would prohibit them from joining in the Passover celebrations. They would not therefore enter the judgement hall in Pilate's palace, so he came out to see them. He told them to judge Jesus according to their own law, but the Jews said that they were not permitted to put a man to death. They accused him of perverting the nation, and claiming to be The King. They said he had told people not to pay tribute money to Caesar, which was not true. Jesus did not try to defend himself, as it was not his intention to justify himself, but his purpose was rather to go to the cross. Caiaphas asked him if he was the King of the Jews, and Jesus said that he was, but his kingdom was not of this world. He had come into the world to bring the truth to those who would listen. Pilate did not want to find out what the truth was, but he could find no fault with Jesus, so went outside to where the Jews were waiting, and told them so.

It so happened that Herod, ruler of Galilee and Perea, was in Jerusalem at that time. When Pilate found out that Jesus was from Galilee, he decided to send him to Herod. Herod was quite happy to see Jesus as he had heard about

CHAPTER SEVEN

the miracles, and was looking forward to seeing one himself. He questioned him at length, but Jesus did not say anything, so Herod and his men began to mock him. They wrapped him in a fancy robe, then sent him back to Pilate.

Judas Iscariot heard about what was happening to Jesus, and the realisation of what he had done suddenly hit him. He went to the chief priests and elders in the temple, and told them that betraying Jesus had been wrong, for he was innocent. The Jews were not interested in what he had to say, so Judas threw the thirty pieces of silver on the floor, and left. He felt desperate and alone, and there was no one with whom he could talk. He left the city and headed south to the valley of Hinnom, and arrived at a field called the "Potter's Field". This was the place where Jeremiah had broken the clay pot to symbolise the broken state which Israel was in, and where he had prophesied that disaster would come to Israel because of their sin (Jeremiah 19). Judas found a suitable tree, and climbed it. He was going to hang himself, probably by using his belt. Comparing the account of his death in Acts 1 with that in Matthew 27, it would seem that his hanging body fell from the tree, and onto the ground below. It must have landed on something sharp, like a rock, and burst open, and his intestines spilled out. Back in the city, the priests were wondering what to do with the thirty pieces of silver Judas had left on the temple floor. It would not have been right to put it in the temple treasury, as it was blood money. The money still legally belonged to Judas, so they decided to buy the Potter's Field in the name of Judas, and use it as a burial ground for strangers. It became known as the Field of Blood.

In the judgement hall, Pilate once again had the problem of what to do with Jesus. It was the custom on that feast day for the Roman governor to release a prisoner who had been condemned to death, and a large crowd of people had gathered outside to watch. Pilate had an idea. He did not want to put Jesus to death, so he suggested to the Jews that he would scourge him, then release him, for he had to release one prisoner that day. He was surprised when they did not accept his offer, but the chief priests and scribes had stirred up the people to shout for the release of another prisoner, called Barabbas.

Pilate then sat down on the judgement seat, but before he could pass sentence, someone came to him with a message from his wife. She had had a disturbing dream, and she said to her husband, "Don't have anything to do with that innocent man" (Matthew 27:19). The crowd were still shouting for the release of Barabbas, so Pilate asked them what he should do with Jesus. "Crucify him," they cried, but Pilate asked them what Jesus had done to deserve that. The people cried out all the more, and Pilate could see that he was not able to reason with them, so he decided to opt out of the situation. He called for a bowl of water, and washed his hands before the people, as a symbol that he was washing his hands of the whole affair. He was determined to be innocent himself, but, in reality, he was giving the crowd what they wanted. He released Barabbas, and sent Jesus to be scourged.

This was a cruel punishment. The prisoner was stripped, and his hands were tied behind his back. He was beaten with a 'scourge', which was a whip of leather strips imbedded with spikes. It tore the flesh off the poor victim. This was what Jesus had to endure now. Afterwards, the soldiers took Jesus back to the judgement hall, where they made fun of him, and dressed him up like a king. They gave him a purple robe and made him a crown of thorns. They put a reed in his right hand for a sceptre. "Hail King

CHAPTER SEVEN

of the Jews", they shouted. They mocked him, by pretending to worship him, they struck him on the head with the reed and spat at him. Pilate made a final appeal to the Jews, but they insisted that Jesus must be crucified. They did not accept that he was the Son of God. Pilate sat down at the judgement seat once more. Out of fear, Pilate ordered Jesus to be taken away and crucified.

The soldiers took off the purple robe and gave Jesus back his own clothes. Then they led him to Golgotha, the place of the crucifixion. This was situated outside the city walls, and to the northwest. Jesus must have been exhausted, as he had not had any sleep that night, and he had not eaten since the supper the evening before, but he had to carry his own cross on his back. With him walked two thieves, who were also going to be crucified that day, and behind them, a large crowd of onlookers was gathering. When they got to the city walls, Jesus must have collapsed under the weight of his cross. A man called Simon, from Cyrene in Africa, happened to be walking towards the crowd, so the soldiers stopped him, and forced him to carry the cross for Jesus, who was now so weak that he had to have help walking the rest of the way to Golgotha. The women who had followed the procession, were now crying, so Jesus turned to them and told them not to weep for him, but for themselves and their children. They would surely suffer in the judgement that was coming to Israel.

At nine o'clock in the morning, Jesus was put on the cross at Golgotha. The two thieves were crucified, one on the right, and one on the left of Jesus. Some Jews offered Jesus a drink, but when he realised that it was a mixture of strong wine and myrrh, he refused to take it. He did not want to dull his senses. He wanted to suffer the punishment for our sins in full. At this point, Jesus cried out, "Father forgive them, for they do not what they are doing" (Luke 23:34). This was the first of the seven 'cries of the cross' as they are sometimes called, referring to the seven times Jesus spoke while he was on the cross. Then the soldiers divided his clothes between them, but cast lots to see who would get his coat. It was a seamless coat, and they did not want to tear it into pieces. As the disciple John stood there, he could see the prophecy of Psalm 22:18 coming true. "They divide my garments among them and cast lots for my clothing."

Pilate had written an inscription, and this was nailed above the Lord's head. It read, "This is Jesus the King of the Jews", and it was written in Hebrew, Latin and Greek. The Jews did not like this inscription; they would have preferred it to say that Jesus claimed he was the King of the Jews, but Pilate would not alter it. Then everyone there began to mock the Lord. There were soldiers, Jews, people passing by, and even the two thieves joined in. "He saved others," they said, "but he can't save himself!" (Mark 15:31). "Aren't you the Christ? Save yourself and us!" said one of the thieves, but the other thief rebuked him. "Don't you fear God, he said, …this man has done nothing wrong." Then he said, "Jesus, remember me when you come into your kingdom." Jesus answered him, "I tell you the truth, today you will be with me in paradise" (Luke 23:39-43). One thief would join Jesus in heaven, but the other would not.

It is likely that the apostle John had brought the Galilean women to the scene of the crucifixion. Amongst them was Mary the mother of Jesus, her sister Salome (John's mother), and her sister-in law, (also called Mary). Mary Magdalene was also there. When Jesus saw his mother standing near the cross, he uttered his third cry, "Dear woman, here is your son" (John 19:26). Then he looked at John and said, "Here is your mother" (John 19:27).

CHAPTER SEVEN

John knew that Jesus wanted him to look after Mary from now on, and so he took her away from the cross. The other women moved away from the cross too, although they did not leave the scene completely. It was now midday, and Jesus had been on the cross for three hours. Suddenly it went dark, and stayed that way for the next three hours. During this time, the Lord's suffering was most acute. As well as the physical pain, he was suffering in his spirit too, as he was totally alone at this point. Even God had abandoned him. Psalm 22 helps us to understand a little of his anguish, as he bore our punishment on that cross. At about three o'clock in the afternoon, Jesus expressed his thoughts as he cried out, "Eloi, Eloi, lama sabachthani?" which translated means "My God, my God, why have you forsaken me?" (Mark 15:34). Jews would have recognised this as a quotation from Psalm 22:1, but a Gentile may not, and some of them thought he was calling for Elijah. The fifth cry Jesus uttered was "I am thirsty" (John 19:28). One person offered Jesus a strong drink, which this time he took, then, he said, "It is finished" (John 19:30). Lastly, he cried out with a loud voice, "Father, into your hands I commit my spirit" (Luke 23:46). Then, he gave up his life. He was dead.

As he died, the veil in the temple was torn in two, from the top to the bottom. Beyond the veil was the most holy place in the temple, where the High Priest went only once a year. By tearing the veil in two, God was saying that from now on, anyone could approach him, at any time. God also demonstrated his power as the earth quaked and the graves of believers were opened. (After the resurrection, these resurrected bodies appeared to many people in Jerusalem. When the Lord returned to heaven, they no doubt accompanied him there.) These wonders caused the centurion who was guarding Jesus to state that "Surely this man was the Son of God!" (Mark 15:39). The Galilean women and other followers of Jesus stood watching from a distance, but Mary the mother of Jesus had already left.

The sunset would bring the commencement of the Sabbath, and as it was also the Passover time, this Sabbath was called a 'high-day'. The Jews needed to make preparations to celebrate the Passover, so they asked Pilate if they could bury the three men now, rather than leave them hanging on the crosses. It was against their law to leave dead bodies hanging overnight (Deuteronomy 21:22-23). Pilate allowed this, and the soldiers went to take down the bodies. The custom was for the soldiers to break the bones of the victims with a club or a hammer, which increased their pain. Then they would pierce them with a sword or a spear, which ended their suffering and their life. This was what happened to the two thieves, but when the soldiers came to Jesus, he was dead already, so they did not break his bones. One of the soldiers pierced the Lord's side with a spear, and blood and water came out. The apostle John saw the significance in all these things as he stood there watching. Old Testament prophecies, which stated that his bones would not be broken, but he would be pierced, were coming true at that very moment. Later, in his first epistle, John talks more about the water and the blood (1 John 5).

Joseph of Arimathea was a respected and wealthy member of the Jewish council. He was a righteous man, and he had disagreed with the decision to condemn Jesus, as he was secretly a disciple. He had gone to Pilate and asked him if he could have the body of Jesus, so he could bury him in his own tomb, which was cut out of the rock in a nearby garden. Pilate was surprised that Jesus was dead already, as crucifixion was a slow death, but he did not understand

CHAPTER SEVEN

that the Lord had voluntarily given up his life, when he was ready. As Creator, God has control over life itself. Joseph was permitted to take the body, so he bought some fine linen for covering the body, and Nicodemus, another previously secret disciple, brought spices for the burial. And so it was that Jesus was buried, in a brand new tomb, in a garden, in Jerusalem. A large stone was placed at the entrance to the tomb. A few of the Galilean women had followed discreetly to see what was happening, and where they were taking Jesus.

On the Saturday, the chief priests and Pharisees suggested to Pilate that he place some guards at the tomb. They were worried that the disciples might come and steal Jesus' body, and claim that he had risen from the dead. Pilate agreed to the suggestion, and so the tombstone was sealed and guarded.

Chapter Eight

At sunrise on the Sunday morning, Mary Magdalene, Mary the wife of Clopas and Salome came back to the tomb, bringing with them spices and ointments for anointing the Lord's body. They mustn't have realised that this had already been done. They wondered who would roll away the stone from the tomb, as it would be too heavy for them to move. When they arrived there, they saw that the stone had already been rolled away from the entrance to the tomb. The guards looked terrified, and

CHAPTER EIGHT

could not speak. Mary Magdalene rushed off to find Peter and John. She told them that she did not know where Jesus was; his body had gone. The men seemed to believe her, and ran as fast as they could to the tomb. John was a faster runner, and got there first. He looked into the tomb and saw the empty linen cloths. Peter then arrived at the tomb and went straight inside. He too saw the linen cloths, and the napkin that had covered the Lord's head. This was now folded up neatly. John followed him in, and he believed that Jesus had risen from the dead. Peter did not seem quite so sure at this stage. The two disciples then returned to the place where they were staying.

Mary Magdalene returned to the tomb, weeping. She bent down and looked inside the tomb, and saw two angels, one sitting where Jesus' head had been, and one where his feet had been. They asked her why she was crying, and she told them that she did not know where the body of Jesus was. It had gone. Then she turned round, and in the garden, she saw a man standing there. "Woman," he said, "why are you crying? Who is it you are looking for?" (John 20:15). The man was Jesus, but Mary thought it was the gardener, and she asked him if he had moved Jesus' body. He answered only "Mary", then she recognised his voice. She knew it was the Lord. She wanted to touch him, but he explained to her that the relationship between himself and his followers had now changed from an earthly to a spiritual relationship. This spiritual relationship would begin after Jesus had ascended into heaven. In the meantime, Mary was not allowed to touch him. Mary accepted what Jesus had said. Then he asked her to go to his followers, and tell them that she had seen him, and that he was going to return to his Father, and theirs. Sadly, the people she told did not believe her.

Some of the other Galilean women had also returned to the tomb. They too had seen that the stone was no longer blocking the tomb entrance. There had been some sort of earthquake, and the Angel of the Lord had rolled back the stone from the tomb. The appearance of the angel, shining and white, was frightening the women, so the angel told them not to be afraid. Jesus was no longer in the tomb, he was risen. He showed them the place where the body had been, and reminded the women that Jesus had told them he would rise again on the third day. He then told them to go and tell the disciples that the Lord was risen and he would meet them back in Galilee. They ran out of the tomb, feeling both frightened and ecstatic, and on their way to find the disciples, Jesus came to meet them. They bowed down at his feet and worshipped him. He told them not to be afraid but to tell the disciples that he would see them all in Galilee.

By now the guards had composed themselves enough to report what they had seen to the chief priests in the city. The Jewish council met, and they decided to bribe the soldiers into claiming that the disciples had stolen Jesus' body overnight. They told the soldiers that they would protect them if their governor found out about this. They gladly took the money, and spread the false report.

After this, the Lord appeared to two more of his followers, Clopas and his wife. This couple had left Jerusalem, and were walking to a village called Emmaus, which was about seven miles outside the city. On the way, they discussed all that had been happening that day. Jesus joined them on the road, but they did not realise that it was he. He asked them what they were discussing. Clopas wondered where this man had been. Had he not heard the news? Did he not realise what had happened in Jerusalem that day? They looked so sad. If only they had known that Jesus was

CHAPTER EIGHT

with them! They told the 'stranger' how Jesus the Mighty Prophet had been crucified three days ago, but now his body had gone. Some women they knew had seen angels, who said that Jesus was alive, but they had not seen him. Then Jesus, without telling them who he was, taught them how the Old Testament spoke of Christ and how he would suffer and die, and enter into glory.

The journey soon passed and they arrived at Emmaus. The day was nearly over, and the couple insisted that the 'stranger' came back to their house. They had been fascinated by what he had said, and wanted to spend some more time with him. They prepared some simple food, and sat down to eat. Jesus took the bread, blessed it and broke it, and shared it out. Suddenly their eyes were opened, and they realised that it was the Lord. Then he vanished from their sight. They recalled the wonderful time they had spent with him on the road, when he had explained the scriptures to them. Even though they had not known Jesus was with them at the time, their hearts had burned within them, as the scriptures were opened up to them. We too can appreciate the Lord through the scriptures, even though we cannot physically see him.

At some point in the day, Jesus also appeared to Simon Peter, although we do not know any details of what took place. Having denied the Lord three times, Peter would no doubt appreciate this time alone with the Lord.

The two believers from Emmaus were so excited about having spent time with the Lord, that they left and headed straight back to Jerusalem. They found the disciples and other followers altogether in one place. They were afraid of what the Jews might do to them, and so had gathered together for safety. The disciple Thomas was not with them at this time. As they were speaking, Jesus came to them and stood amongst them. "Peace be with you!" he said (John 20:19). They were all terrified, and thought they had seen a ghost. Jesus asked them what was wrong, and he showed them his hands, feet and side, where the scars were. He was not a ghost, as he had flesh and bones that they could touch. He then joined them in a meal, again proving that he was no ghost. They were confused, as they wanted to believe what they were seeing, but they did not dare.

Jesus then taught them all about how the Old Testament spoke of him, just as he had explained to the two on the road to Emmaus. They began to understand what he was saying, as he had "opened their minds" (Luke 24:45). After this, he reminded them of the need for the Gospel to be preached in Jerusalem first, then throughout the world. Then he breathed on them, and said, "Receive the Holy Spirit" (John 20:22). This receiving of the Holy Spirit would enable them to carry out their service for him. (At Pentecost, in only a few weeks time, the Holy Spirit would come down from heaven, and indwell all believers in the Lord Jesus Christ.) In this room was the beginning of the church. They were to preach, and baptise believers. The Holy Spirit would enable them to cast out demons and speak in any language. They would be able to heal the sick in Jesus' name. These powers were given to the early church as signs to the world. This period from now until Pentecost, when the Holy Spirit would come in full to all believers, would be a unique time in the history of the church.

As soon as the disciples saw Thomas again, they told him what he had missed. Thomas wanted to see Jesus for himself; he wanted to touch him and see his scars before he believed that he was alive. A week later, the disciples were all gathered together, and this time Thomas was with

CHAPTER EIGHT

them. They had shut the door of the room. Once again, Jesus suddenly appeared amongst them. "Peace be with you!" he said (John 20:26). He looked at Thomas and invited him to come and see and touch his hands and side. Thomas felt ashamed at his unbelief. "My Lord and my God!" he answered (John 20:28). He was acknowledging the full Deity of Jesus. Thomas the doubter was left in no doubt at all that Jesus was the Son of God. "Because you have seen me, you have believed; blessed are those who have not seen and yet have believed," said Jesus (John 20:29).

Now that the Passover celebrations were over, the disciples returned to Galilee. Presumably, the Galilean women travelled back with them. Jesus had said that he would see them in Galilee, so they must have been looking forward to that. One night, seven of the disciples went fishing on the Sea of Galilee. Simon Peter, Thomas, Nathaniel, James and John were there, and also two other disciples. They fished all night, but caught nothing. (Peter, James and John must have remembered the time when they were called to be apostles. On that occasion, they had unsuccessfully fished all night too, but Jesus came along and told them to take their boat out again. They obeyed, and went on to catch a net full of fish.) Now it was morning, and as they were coming back in, Jesus appeared on the shore, but they did not recognise him. "Friends, haven't you any fish?" he shouted (John 21:5). They answered that they had nothing, so Jesus told them to cast their net on the right side of the boat, and they would find fish. They obeyed, and the net became so full of fish, that they could not lift it.

Now John realised that it was Jesus, and said this to Simon Peter, who immediately jumped out of the boat, into the water, and waded ashore. The others got into a smaller boat and rowed to the shore, dragging the net of fish with them. On the beach, Jesus had prepared a coal fire, and was cooking some fish. The disciples quietly approached Jesus, and he told them to bring their fish up, so Simon Peter went to drag the net up the beach. The fish were so large that they decided to count them, and found that there were one hundred and fifty three of them. They shared the breakfast that Jesus had made, and afterwards Jesus spoke to Simon Peter. As Peter had denied the Lord three times, Jesus wanted to put this matter to rest once and for all, so he asked him three questions. Each question was the same, "Simon son of John, do you truly love me?" (John 21:16). Peter answered that of course he did, so Jesus told him to "Take care of my sheep" (John 21:16). He wanted him to care for the people of God. The Lord wanted to make sure that Peter would not be inhibited in his service for him because of those three denials. It was time to move on, and there was work to do. He also told Peter that he would eventually be martyred. Then Jesus told Peter to follow him, so he got up, and John followed too. Peter noticed this, and asked Jesus what was going to

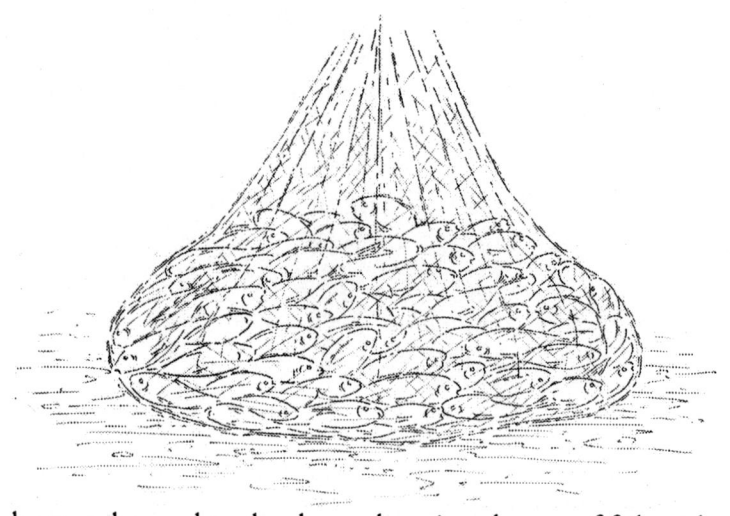

CHAPTER EIGHT

happen to John. Jesus replied that it was not really his business whether John lived for many years or not; the important thing was that Peter and John would both be able to serve the Lord in their own ways. Peter would become a great preacher, and John would become a great teacher.

1 Corinthians 15:6-7 tell us that Jesus also appeared to five hundred believers at once, and then he saw his brother James, who had recently been converted. James went on to be the head of the first Christian church, and he wrote the epistle of James. During the forty days that the Lord was on earth, after his resurrection, he taught the disciples as much as he could. He met them all on a mountain in Galilee, and reminded them of their commission to go into the nations and preach, teach and baptise. He would always be with them, even to the end of the world.

Jesus was now ready to return to heaven, so he travelled back down to Jerusalem with the disciples. He led them up the Mount of Olives as far as Bethany. He told them to stay in Jerusalem for a while, until the Holy Spirit should come. It would not be long now. As he was speaking to them, he lifted up his hands to bless them, and a cloud came down and carried the Lord up to heaven. The disciples watched him go, and stared into the sky. Then they noticed two men dressed in white, standing by them. They were angels. "Men of Galilee," they said, "why do you stand here looking into the sky? This same Jesus, who has been taken from you into heaven, will come back in the same way you have seen him go into heaven" (Acts 1:11). Then the disciples returned to Jerusalem with great joy, and were continually in the temple, praising and blessing God.

JESUS – A TRUE STORY

Bibliography

The Life and Times of Jesus the Messiah by Alfred Edersheim

Harmony of the Gospels by Benjamin Davies

Handbook to the Bible (New Testament) by Walter Scott

The Gospel in the Feasts of Israel by Victor Buksbazen

Expository Dictionary of New Testament Words by W. E. Vine

Notes

CHAPTER ONE

1. Was Jesus really born on 25th December? According to Edersheim, "There is no adequate reason for questioning the historical accuracy of this date". (*The Life and Times of Jesus the Messiah*, volume 1, chapter 6.)

2. These sheep were destined for temple sacrifices, and were kept outside all year round.

3. It is generally taken that it was baby boys only that were killed, and not the girls. As Bethlehem was only a small town, it would not have been a large number of boys, maybe twenty.

CHAPTER TWO

1. The Sabbath was the Jews' holy day, and was on a Saturday.

2. John might have stayed with the Lord at the well, as he is the only Gospel writer to tell us of this incident. Some people think that this happened at noon. This depends on whether John was using Jewish or Roman time. The Jews calculated time in

two twelve-hour blocks, from sunset to sunset (6.00pm) so the new day began at sunset. The first hour in the evening was what we would now call 7.00pm. In the morning, the first hour was what we would call 7.00am, so the sixth hour would be noon. Roman time is the same as the time we use today, where the sixth hour means six o'clock, either morning or evening. It is generally regarded that John wrote in Roman time, and Matthew, Mark and Luke wrote using Jewish time.

3. Some writers think that this unspecified feast (John 5:1) was a Passover feast, but the Bible does not say that it was this feast. If it was the Passover, then there is a gap from the summer until the following March/April when the Passover would be. This means that we know nothing of what Jesus did in all this time.

4. The Pharisees were a strict Jewish sect.

Chapter Three

1. Scribes were teachers of Jewish Law

2. Gentiles are non-Jewish people.

3. Jews regarded the houses of Gentiles as unclean.

4. The exact nature of the disease is not clear.

5. The literal Greek translation of the word rank is prasia, meaning a garden plot. This gives us the picture of them all looking like a huge garden of flowers; it must have been quite a sight.

6. Washing before a meal was an important Jewish ritual.

NOTES

7. Some writers think that there were four Passovers in the Lord's public ministry, in which case this one would be the third.

8. Picking corn on the Sabbath was against Jewish laws.

9. Herodians were a political party who followed Herod.

10. The Sadducees were a Jewish sect who did not believe in the resurrection.

CHAPTER FOUR

1. The Kingdom of Heaven refers to the time in the future when Jesus will reign over the earth.

2. The word dine used here is the Greek word aristao, which means the first meal of the day, or breakfast, so this meal would have been the following morning, or maybe even a few days later.

3. This feast celebrated the time in 164 BC when the temple was rededicated after having been ransacked by Antiochus Epiphanes, ruler of Syria, in 169 BC. The feast was held on 25th December.

CHAPTER SEVEN

1. Edersheim regards the seat to the left of the head of the company as the best. For further reading, see *The Life and Times of Jesus the Messiah*, volume 2, chapter 10.

Printed in the United Kingdom
by Lightning Source UK Ltd.
116511UKS00001B/103-138